Praise for *Process Design*

"I have finally found a wonderful reference book that captures all the little pieces of the puzzle that must come together for an effective process design. If only I had this book fifteen years ago, it would have saved light years of learning!"

—**Kristin J. Arnold**, president, Quality Process Consultants, Inc.

"A true gift to all those who refuse to leave success to chance. This guide respectfully acknowledges the complex dynamics of group interactions and the precision required of facilitators to create flawless events."

—**Tracy Thurkow**, partner, CLG Inc.

"I highly recommend this book to anyone who facilitates, which is everyone! Whether you are a professional facilitator or novice, the practical tips and tools in this book will enhance any session you run."

—**Christopher Whitnall**, director, Talkforce Consulting, Australia

PROCESS DESIGN

Making It Work

A Practical Guide to What to Do
When and How for Facilitators,
Consultants, Managers, and Coaches

DOROTHY STRACHAN
PAUL TOMLINSON

JOSSEY-BASS
A Wiley Company
San Francisco

Published by Jossey-Bass
A Wiley Imprint
989 Market Street, San Francisco, CA 94103-1741—www.josseybass.com

Jossey-Bass books and products are available through most bookstores. To contact Jossey-Bass directly call our Customer Care Department within the U.S. at 800-956-7739, outside the U.S. at 317-572-3986, or fax 317-572-4002.

Jossey-Bass also publishes its books in a variety of electronic formats. Some content that appears in print may not be available in electronic books.

Library of Congress Cataloging-in-Publication Data

Strachan, Dorothy.
  Process Design: Making it work, a practical guide to what to do when and how for facilitators, consultants, managers, and coaches / Dorothy Strachan and Paul Tomlinson.
       p. cm.
  Includes bibliographical references.
  ISBN 978-0-470-18270-3 (pbk.)
  1. Group facilitation. 2. Planning. I. Tomlinson, Paul. II. Title.
  HM751.S767 2008
  658.5'1—dc22
                                                                        2008003847

Printed in the United States of America
FIRST EDITION
PB Printing 10 9 8 7 6 5 4 3 2 1

The Jossey-Bass Business & Management Series

Contents

Acknowledgments

There is enough to learn about process consulting to last a lifetime. And it has taken the better part of a lifetime for us to gain the experience to write this book. A heartfelt thank-you to all the colleagues, clients, stakeholders, and process participants who taught us important lessons along the way.

Several years ago we held three focus groups with experienced facilitators to kick off the writing process for this book. Participants' enthusiasm for the topic and their sense of humor were invaluable. Thank you to each group member who participated in these discussions—Sylvie Bigras, Brenda Buchanan, Susan Carlton, Brenda Chartrand, Carmen Connolly, Peggy Edwards, Julie Francisco, Sibyl Frei, Wanda Généreux, Sylvia Laale, Lise Lamontagne, Sue Potter, Nora Sheffe, Mary Jane Sterne, Linda Vanderlee, Sarah Chen Wing, and Lisa Weiss, who also contributed her research skills to the development of this book.

Special thanks to Brian Benn and members of the Ontario Public Service Facilitators' Network who participated in a two-day pilot workshop on process design and provided helpful feedback on an earlier draft. Your candid input and perceptive comments are much appreciated!

Several reviewers responded generously to a request for comments. Their constructive insights and support for the contribution of this book to the profession of process consulting buoyed us up when the road looked particularly long. Our sincere appreciation goes to Kristin J. Arnold, Pamela Fitch, Leigh Passman, Marian Pitters, Roger Schwarz, Cresswell Walker, and Christopher Whitnall.

It has been a particular pleasure to work with Sam Shemie and Kimberly Young on collaborative, national consensus-building processes to support the important work of the Canadian Council for Donation and Transplantation. Our experience as team members over several years is reflected in the case described in Chapters Fifteen and Seventeen.

We would also like to acknowledge Albert Prisner (Ottawa) for the artwork in the book.

The best editors play a significant role in shaping a final manuscript. Through their perceptive feedback, Mary Garrett and Hilary Powers significantly enhanced our final product. Kathe Sweeney, senior editor for business and management at Jossey-Bass, merits a special mention for her exceptional analytical skills, positive support, and ongoing commitment to produce the best book possible.

January 2008
Ottawa, Canada

Dorothy Strachan
Paul Tomlinson

The Authors

Dorothy Strachan and Paul Tomlinson are partners in Strachan-Tomlinson, an Ottawa-based process consulting firm. They have been working as full-time process consultants since 1974, serving clients across the public, nonprofit, and private sectors in several countries.

In addition to her consulting work, Dorothy enjoys creating and delivering learning-centered training sessions on process design, facilitation, and conscious questioning. Participants in these workshops want to expand their skills in working with groups effectively: they are professional process consultants as well as managers, coaches, facilitators, administrators, and educators. (For more information, visit www.strachan-tomlinson.com.) Paul's specialty is in gathering and developing the background information and concepts that inform Strachan-Tomlinson's process consulting work. His background in adult education has been an important element in building the company's learning-centered approaches to group process and organizational change.

Process Design: Making It Work is a companion book to *Making Questions Work* by Dorothy Strachan, published by Jossey-Bass in 2007. Both these resources are based on many years' experience and are filled with hundreds of practice guidelines, tips, and suggestions based on real-life examples. The "we" in this book refers to Paul and Dorothy.

There is an African proverb that it takes a community to raise a child. In a similar vein, it took a family to write this book. And so as parents we dedicate this book to Mike and Jesse Tomlinson in appreciation for their enthusiastic support and insightful reviews.

Process
Design

Introduction

When we first developed workshop agendas in the 1970s and '80s, most participants were excited to be involved and open to whatever an agenda might deliver. They exhibited a refreshing openness to group process and welcomed the opportunity to try techniques such as brainstorming for the first time.

It's much different today. Most of the clients, stakeholders, and process participants we encounter have considerable experience with group process and also have opinions about how an agenda should flow and what should be done during each part of a process. When you combine this situation with the fact that more and more work is being done collaboratively in groups, teams, and workshops, it is clear that expectations have risen significantly.

The "you" in this book refers to facilitators, consultants, managers, and coaches who work with people to get things done in group situations. You may be an internal organizational leader or manager, an external process consultant (facilitator and designer), coach, or someone who wants to engage an external consultant in process design and facilitation and needs to know more about what is involved in that work. This book addresses the challenge of how to create process designs that really work for you and for your clients, stakeholders, and participants.

THEMES

Five themes anchor this book:

1. *A stepwise approach to process design results in a complete and thorough description of what needs to happen in a process to achieve required outcomes.* Part One describes key steps and related guidelines for developing process designs. Chapter One details six steps:

  a. Complete a process terms of reference (PTR).

  b. Block the agenda.

  c. Develop and confirm the agenda flow.

  d. Build a preliminary design.

  e. Check the preliminary design.

  f. Complete the design.

Chapter Two provides practical suggestions for implementing these six steps.

2. *People are the key ingredient in process designs that achieve expected outcomes.* The three chapters in Part Two explore important influencers that affect how people participate in a process: individual perspectives, the types of power held by individuals and groups, and differences in values.

3. *Organizations, agencies, partnerships, networks, and alliances are complex entities. Understanding this complexity is a prerequisite to effective design and facilitation.* Part Three describes eight elements in a comprehensive framework for developing the up-front work required to inform successful design and facilitation. Chapter Six describes the role that a "process terms of reference" (PTR) plays in laying the groundwork for developing a design. Each of the eight subsequent chapters explores one element in a PTR, as indicated by their titles:

  • Chapter Seven, "Understanding the Situation"

  • Chapter Eight, "Developing a Focus"

  • Chapter Nine, "Stakeholder Collaboration"

  • Chapter Ten, "Core Assumptions"

- Chapter Eleven, "Key Considerations"
- Chapter Twelve, "Work Plan"
- Chapter Thirteen, "Governance"
- Chapter Fourteen, "Essential Documents"

The last chapter in Part Three outlines three examples of PTR documents completed for different situations and sectors.

4. *Evidence-based processes present unique design challenges, particularly when it comes to developing the questions that drive them.* The two chapters in Part Four discuss and illustrate ways to make evidence-based questions work effectively in these designs.

5. *The essence of effective design and facilitation is customization: no one best method, tool, approach, technology, or model works for most situations.* Part Five provides a pair of customized process designs to address different situations. Each design integrates a range of models, methods, tools, techniques, and resources to enable achievement of its purpose and objectives.

ABOUT THE WORD *PROCESS*

The word *process* is used in a number of different ways in various systems. Here is how we use it in this book.

> *Process:* A continuous series of actions and events set up to accomplish something with a group. Processes are dynamic: they have their own unique origins, lengths, developmental cycles, and conclusions. A process may be a single workshop that happens over a few hours or a longer initiative that includes a series of meetings, consultations, and reports that take place over eighteen months or longer. This book focuses on how to design a major process—such as a workshop, forum, consultation, retreat, conference think tank, or summit—within a large, multiphase initiative.

> *Process Consulting:* An expertise that enables people working together (in teams, groups, departments, organizations, communities, regions, or countries) to develop and realize the purpose and objectives of an initiative. Understanding the process consultant role is essential for leaders and managers, internal and external organizational change specialists, human resource personnel, coaches, educators, and others engaged in enabling others to work together toward specific goals.

Process consulting encompasses two distinct but related functions: *design* (the primary focus of this book), in which a flow of deliberately sequenced activities leads to projected outcomes, and *facilitation,* in which you attend to group process as people participate in those activities. The development and facilitation of a broad range of process designs, each of which is complex in its own way, demands an integrated approach to design and facilitation.

> In its broadest sense "process" refers to *how* things are done rather than *what* is done. If I am crossing the street, that is what I am doing, but the process is how I am crossing: walking, running, dodging cars, asking someone to help me across because I feel dizzy. Process is everywhere. In order to help, intervene, and facilitate human problem solving, one must focus on communication and interpersonal processes. The processes we need to learn to observe and manage are those that make a demonstrable difference to problem solving, decision-making, and organizational effectiveness in general.
>
> —Schein, 1987, p 39.

ABOUT PROPOSITIONS

Propositions are provided at the end of each chapter to stimulate further reflection and learning about how the values, assumptions, and considerations of process design and facilitation are reflected in the reality of day-to-day practice.

4

Each statement is a proposition to the extent that it expresses a judgment or opinion of the authors. Each statement is about learning to the extent that it invites further reflection, investigation, and discussion. As Aristotle put it, "It is the mark of an educated mind to entertain a thought without accepting it."

INVESTING IN PROCESS DESIGN

Facilitated processes are expensive in many ways. When you tally the time, energy, and money involved in the simplest initiatives, it takes real work and a significant effort focused on outcomes to ensure that projected benefits offset the various costs of process design.

A senior manager in a high-tech company did a quick calculation of his company's investment in a one-day team development workshop for his group. When he included time off and salaries for committee work; staff participation in the session (fifteen people); travel and accommodation for a site about twenty-five miles from work; workshop room rental; breakfast, lunch, dinner, and breaks for everyone; preparation of background documents; audiovisual supplies; a process consultant and workshop report writer; and human resource department expenses related to rearranging work schedules to cover absent employees, the cost was around US$50,000. And this estimate didn't include the personal costs to employees for challenges such as rearranging their home lives, paying for child care, or rescheduling family obligations.

Given the investments required for success, it is essential to ensure that a comprehensive approach is in place to support the creation of productive, enjoyable, and dynamic processes that really work for stakeholders. This comprehensive approach is the focus of this book.

When you work at it, it works.

A STEPWISE APPROACH

The word *stepwise* evokes two ideas: developing a process design involves separate and essential steps, and it takes wisdom to determine how these steps will be organized and implemented.

The process consultant (designer and facilitator) determines the direction, order, and pacing of these steps to support progress toward outcomes. Sometimes a client is clear about parts of Step 3 (deciding how the agenda will flow) and wants to discuss that before Step 1 (constructing a process terms of reference) is in place. Sometimes two steps will happen almost simultaneously; other times one step will need to be broken down into what may seem to be baby steps that will take place gradually over a period of time. Customizing the steps to meet the needs of each situation puts the "wise" into stepwise.

1 Six Steps

A process may be a single workshop that happens over a few hours or a longer initiative that includes a series of meetings, strategic sessions, consultations, and reports that take place over eighteen months or more. This book focuses on how to design a major process—a workshop, forum, consultation, retreat, conference, think tank, summit, or the like—within a large multiphase initiative.

A stepwise approach to process design recognizes six fundamental steps required to do this work well (Figure 1.1).

Although these six steps are distinct and provide an overall pattern, they are not always taken in this sequence: they interact, overlap, and may seem to converge when an important issue is being discussed. While some steps are more comprehensive

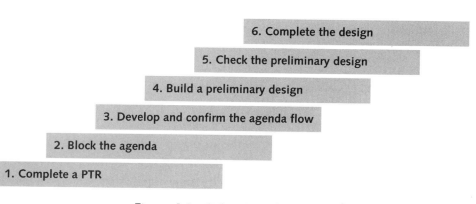

Figure 1.1. A Stepwise Approach

and time-consuming than others, each is an essential and important part of developing a design.

Process designs can be *pre-structured* (thought through ahead of time), *emergent* (thought through on the spot), or some *combination of the two*. Expect the unexpected: it's common to have developed a design for part of a process and then to revise it in response to the demands of the situation.

The more information facilitators have about the situations they face, the better prepared they are to anticipate and address what may happen unpredictably in the resulting processes.

STEP 1. COMPLETE A PROCESS TERMS OF REFERENCE

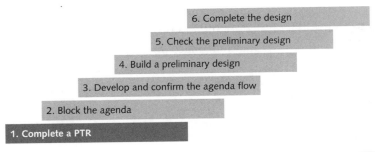

A process terms of reference (PTR) is a conceptual framework for understanding eight key elements that affect how a design rolls out in the hands of a facilitator. These eight elements describe the situation, purpose and objectives, stakeholders, core assumptions, key considerations, work plan, governance, and documentation for an initiative (Figure 1.2).

Completing a PTR with stakeholders enables a disciplined approach to understanding a situation. It is an excellent way to build ownership among stakeholders for an initiative and encourage long-term engagement to support the achievement of outcomes. A PTR goes through several iterations as people work together, thinking, discussing, and writing their way toward clarity.

Developing a PTR also helps address the hindsight "if only" factor that has a tendency to crop up when you are facilitating: *if only* I had included a comprehensive fact sheet on this issue; *if only* we had invited that group of stakeholders; *if only* I had more sector-specific examples to support this discussion; *if only* I had allotted this group task more time; *if only* I had scheduled the keynote speaker on the second morning instead of the first evening when people needed more time to get to know one another better; *if only* I had chosen a different decision-making model to accommodate this group's participation style; *if only* . . .

A PTR can prevent if-only moments like these by clearly articulating the terms and conditions that guide people's interactions and decision making throughout a facilitated event.

Figure 1.2. PTR at a Glance

1

Processes rarely occur individually: they happen in clusters, existing inside, around, and in relation to other processes in various ways. Even when a process intervention looks like a single workshop, it is actually several processes, each with a life of its own: the committee responsible for planning the workshop has its own process; the group responsible for developing and reviewing the background documents for the workshop has its own process; the implementation group has another process when considering how to act on the workshop conclusions. When designing a workshop or meeting within a larger process, the designer needs to keep in mind how the workshop fits into and supports the larger initiative. Completing a PTR helps to ensure that stakeholders have this comprehensive view of a situation.

See Part Three for a detailed guide to developing a PTR.

STEP 2. BLOCK THE AGENDA

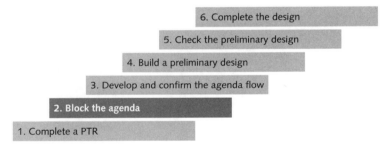

6. Complete the design
5. Check the preliminary design
4. Build a preliminary design
3. Develop and confirm the agenda flow
2. Block the agenda
1. Complete a PTR

An *agenda* is a basic, timed outline for what will happen in a session or workshop process. A *design* is a detailed description of how a session or workshop process will be facilitated.

Using the PTR as a starting point, confirm the basic schedule for the agenda such as starting and finishing times, required opening and closing remarks, meals and breaks, recreation opportunities, and planning committee meetings. Find out if this client group prefers certain timing based on people's participation styles. For example, do they like to have shorter lunches and finish earlier or longer lunches and stay later?

Identify logistical factors that will have an impact on success—people leaving early or coming late, for example, or probable weather challenges. Adjust the basic agenda to accommodate these factors. Be realistic: if people are only going to stay until 3:00 P.M., then don't expect to have an important decision process on the agenda at 3:00 with a finish time scheduled for 4:30.

Although in an ideal situation the process consultant starts from scratch to determine a basic agenda in collaboration with a client or planning committee, what often happens—even before developing a PTR—is that some decisions have already been made such as time available, confirmed speakers, key outputs. If this is the case, be prepared to negotiate the amount of time available for the workshop, keeping in mind the purpose and objectives.

Number the main blocks of working time. One block is usually about an hour and a half to two hours and is framed by breaks and meals. Does the total number of main blocks provide enough time to get the work done?

Be realistic about break times. Most participants have electronic devices with them and will want to check in with their workplace regularly. Given this fact, if you want to have these devices off during a workshop, schedule breaks at least twenty minutes long to enable people to relax a little and also to check their messages.

Identify the best time blocks for optimal learning, energy levels, and decision making. Given what you know about how people will be getting to the workshop, where it will be held, how these processes have happened in the past, and group participation styles, label each block in terms of quality time:

- High = prime, high-quality time when engagement is expected to be highest

- Medium = middle-quality time when engagement needs to be consciously supported

- Low = lower-quality time when productive engagement is least likely

When considering what is prime time, think about how you feel during a process: when you are most likely to be fully engaged and when you are likely to be thinking about other things such as whether the shuttle will arrive in time for you to catch your flight or what time you have to leave in order to pick up your children at day care. Figure 1.3 outlines the probable quality of the blocks in a two-day agenda.

Consider requirements for "fermentation" or "soak" time. Will people be processing substantial amounts of information that can't be integrated in a short time?

1

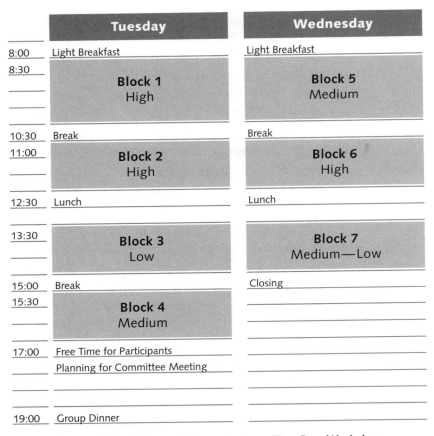

	Tuesday	Wednesday
8:00	Light Breakfast	Light Breakfast
8:30	**Block 1** High	**Block 5** Medium
10:30	Break	Break
11:00	**Block 2** High	**Block 6** High
12:30	Lunch	Lunch
13:30	**Block 3** Low	**Block 7** Medium—Low
15:00	Break	Closing
15:30	**Block 4** Medium	
17:00	Free Time for Participants Planning for Committee Meeting	
19:00	Group Dinner	

Figure 1.3. A Blocked Agenda for a Two-Day Workshop

Identify related initiatives and considerations that may affect participants and therefore how you block the agenda. For example, will people need to start a little later on the first morning because the session you are planning is following another related intense meeting that will be finishing late the evening before?

Encourage your client and key stakeholders to get used to talking

We find the blocks of time after lunch to be the most challenging. People are usually full of food and feeling relaxed, and they need to be engaged at a deep level to get the most out of that time period. Small group work (particularly with groups of three or four people where everyone is involved) supports engagement here.

about blocks of working time. This helps them be realistic about exactly how much time there is for productive work over a designated period. A two-day workshop rarely has more than seven blocks of working time when you take into consideration meals, breaks, and time for recreation and informal networking.

You can create a blocked agenda in ten minutes with your client or planning committee. Avoid getting into a long discussion about this basic outline: it's tempting to get sidetracked into the details of the design when what you need to focus on first is an agenda outline.

STEP 3. DEVELOP AND CONFIRM HOW THE AGENDA WILL FLOW

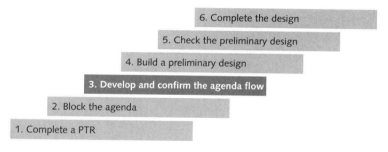

6. Complete the design
5. Check the preliminary design
4. Build a preliminary design
3. Develop and confirm the agenda flow
2. Block the agenda
1. Complete a PTR

The agenda flow outlines the logic for how a process will proceed. It is based primarily on the purpose and objectives as outlined in the PTR.

Dynamic designs are similar to dynamic fitness sessions. Both have three main phases: warmup, workout, and cooldown. Assign the most difficult parts of the process to times when the group is warmed up, and the participants are fairly comfortable with one another and are performing well.

Position other items throughout the agenda based on the nature of activities, choosing time slots according to your priorities: for example, holding interactive group discussions after lunch to support participant engagement. Avoid scheduling key decision-making sessions and turning points at times when participants are likely to be distracted, hungry, or tired.

Include key points about the *warmup* (purpose, outcomes, introductions, norms for working together), the *workout* (where the main objectives will be addressed), and the *cooldown* (concluding remarks, next steps, feedback, debriefing) aspects of the flow.

1

Keep the agenda flow as simple as possible: avoid getting into specific details of the design. Blocking the agenda and describing the flow is about the *what*. The detailed design is about the *how*.

Using Metaphors

Interesting metaphors can make a design come alive. Use the flow of your design to suggest a metaphor that helps people identify with where a process is going and how they can contribute to making it work. A metaphor can also become a creative theme for a day. Some examples:

- "We're a bunch of big heavy whales that are slow to turn. We need to become fast-moving sharks if we want to survive in this industry."
- "We're at the beginning of this process—and based on our background documents, we're pretty much in the ocean here. What we need to do is work together and get into the channel: this is where we want to be this afternoon."
- "Let's think about ourselves as too good and not so good. How are we too good? In what ways are we not so good?"
- "We're hummingbirds now and that's a big part of our success. We're good at hovering over sweet sales and then diving in to get the nectar before our competitors even know it's there."

Encourage participants to make up their own metaphors based on their experience of the challenge they are discussing. Here are two examples of agenda flow, with the metaphor driving the flow:

Flow: yesterday—today—tomorrow (a chronological metaphor)

- Part One: *Yesterday* worldwide—progress to date
- Part Two: *Today* in our country—the current situation
- Part Three: *Tomorrow* across the country—an innovative, integrated system

Flow: information—implications—applications (an input-output metaphor)

- Part One: Provide *information* about what works and doesn't work for joint initiatives.

- Part Two: Explore *implications* of the information in Part One in terms of the purpose and objectives.

- Part Three: Determine *applications* for future joint initiatives.

Creating a visual metaphor to describe the flow gives you a simple and direct way to explain how the agenda will move throughout the workshop. Use it to share ideas with your client and planning committee members, to check that everyone has the same understanding of the process, and to explain the overall approach to participants. Here are some additional common visual metaphors for workshop designs:

- A + B + C = X

- A funnel

- A ladder

- A series of concentric circles

- A star constellation

- A storm leading to a sunny day

- Avoiding bad to worse

- Building blocks for a foundation

- Components leading to an assembled entity

- Confused arrows going in several directions leading to parallel arrows going in a single direction

- Future—past—present; or past—present—future

- Form follows function

- General to specific

- Getting our ducks in a row

- Identify issues—set criteria—choose priorities—set action plan

- Sailing from familiar shores across an unknown sea to distant shores

- Means and ends

- Multiple parts to a single whole

1

- Outside to inside
- Step-by-step
- Synergy: $1 + 1 + 1 = 111$
- Theory into practice
- Venn diagram
- What do you think—what do we think—future thinking
- What works—what doesn't—where to go from here
- Whole-part-whole

Clients and stakeholders often have mental images for a process that remain unconscious until a discussion brings them to the surface. Encourage a creative approach to developing an appropriate visual metaphor. This discussion can also be a useful way to surface inferences about the design: check these out with participants as a way of validating the PTR. Figures 1.4 through 1.13 provide examples of some useful visual metaphors.

If you can't draw the flow and relate it to a metaphor, chances are that: you haven't yet consolidated what the design is about; people are not clear about how the PTR is driving the design; and people are not yet in agreement about what needs to happen to achieve the designated outputs and outcomes.

Maintain a collaborative approach with your client and

Figure 1.4. Avoiding Bad to Worse

Figure 1.5. Bowl Function

Figure 1.6. Broken Circle

Figure 1.7. Ducks in a Row

Figure 1.8. Funnel

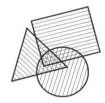

Figure 1.9. Geometric

Figure 1.10. Ladder

Figure 1.11. Sea

Figure 1.12. Sun and Showers

Figure 1.13. Then and Now

planning committee while outlining a flow like the one illustrated in Figure 1.14: this builds ownership for how people participate in the process and follow through on outcomes.

Sometimes clients will have an idea about how to design a session but little training and experience in design. Listen carefully and respect their input, maintaining a collaborative stance while commenting on the risks and benefits of var-

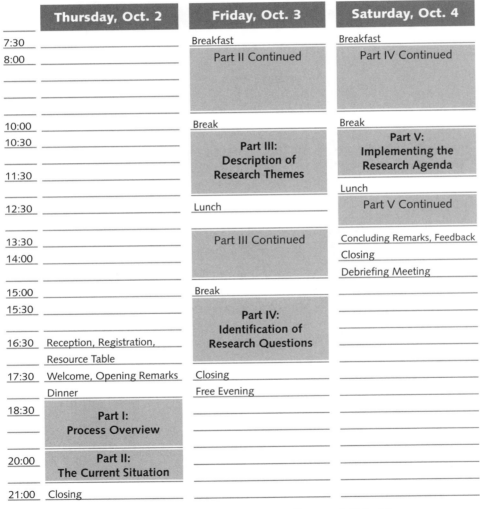

	Thursday, Oct. 2	Friday, Oct. 3	Saturday, Oct. 4
7:30		Breakfast	Breakfast
8:00		Part II Continued	Part IV Continued
10:00		Break	Break
10:30		Part III: Description of Research Themes	Part V: Implementing the Research Agenda
11:30			Lunch
12:30		Lunch	Part V Continued
13:30		Part III Continued	Concluding Remarks, Feedback
14:00			Closing
			Debriefing Meeting
15:00		Break	
15:30		Part IV: Identification of Research Questions	
16:30	Reception, Registration, Resource Table		
17:30	Welcome, Opening Remarks	Closing	
	Dinner	Free Evening	
18:30	Part I: Process Overview		
20:00	Part II: The Current Situation		
21:00	Closing		

Figure 1.14. Agenda Flow: Setting Research Priorities

ious approaches. At the same time, be transparent about your commitment to protecting your ultimate role, responsibility, and accountability for the process design.

For example, in one situation a client proudly told us that he had already done a basic agenda for an issues-based team development process. He had allotted four blocks of time over a two-day period for presentations and discussions on key concepts in team development and three blocks for identifying and discussing issues that team members needed to address.

It was clear that he was quite nervous about getting into difficult conversations and dealing with the potential for people's blaming one another for current problems. By the time we had completed a PTR and revisited the agenda, we had agreed that issues would be identified ahead of time through interviews with team members, and the entire two-day process would be focused on discussing and resolving those issues—with no presentations at all.

STEP 4. BUILD A PRELIMINARY DESIGN

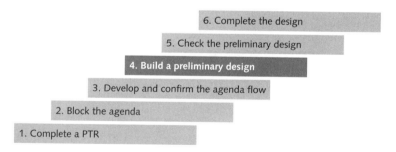

Process frameworks guide the development and flow of process designs. A process framework is a step-by-step conceptual guide to what a facilitator does in a structured group experience. It is like a map organized around facilitation challenges. It makes the process explicit, furnishes a reference point for keeping a process on track, and supports facilitators in thinking about design questions consciously, whether for a single workshop on strategic planning or a long-term, multi-session team development initiative.

Although all processes have their own unique history, situation, objectives, and complicating factors, they also share typical facilitation challenges. Figure 1.15 outlines five process frameworks for five common facilitation challenges. The specific

Opening a Session	Enabling Action	Thinking Critically	Addressing Issues	Closing a Session
1. Getting to know one another 2. Clarifying expectations 3. Building commitment	1. What? (Observation) 2. So what? (Reflection) 3. Now what? (Action)	1. Making assumptions and perspectives explicit 2. Understanding interests and power relationships 3. Exploring alternative ways of thinking and acting 4. Making critical choices	1. Understanding the situation 2. Clarifying the issues 3. Generating options for action 4. Testing options for action 5. Making a decision 6. Taking action	1. Looking backward: wrapping up the process 2. Looking forward: considering the next steps

Figure 1.15. Five Process Frameworks
Strachan, 2007, p. 5.

questions that drive each section of the process framework are outlined in a detailed design.

Every session has a process framework for opening and one for closing. A main process framework such as "addressing issues" forms the basis of a design; sometimes other process frameworks are included as well. To use process frameworks to design a session, think strategically:

- *For the warmup:* Review the process framework for opening a session and decide where you want to put your emphasis in this design. Keep the PTR in mind as you decide on questions and activities.

- *For the workout:* Decide which process frameworks (or combinations of frameworks) you want to use in the main part of the design. For example, you may want to start a strategic planning workshop with people spending some time on questions for critical reflection before moving into the enabling action framework (what—so what—now what).

- *For the cooldown:* Do you want to focus on celebrating success or building ownership for follow-through—or both?

Each preliminary design is customized to fit the unique demands of the PTR its stakeholders have developed. As a result, several models for facilitation are usually integrated in each design. Here is an example of how this might work for a two-day team development workshop:

- *Opening Process Framework:* Open Space model with questions emphasizing expectations and commitment

- *Process Framework for Addressing Issues:* Appreciative Inquiry model for understanding the situation; force field analysis tool to clarify the issues through identification of driving and restraining factors; consensus-building approach to generating and testing options for action; priority-ranking approach to making a decision and taking action

- *Closing Process Framework:* Questions for looking back on the session in terms of learning and productivity and looking forward in terms of the next team development session

---

Checklist: Reviewing a Preliminary Design

The purpose of this checklist is to stimulate additional reflections once you have the preliminary draft of your design in hand.

1. How does the design accommodate the following elements in the PTR? (See Figure 1.2.)

   - *Situation:* Who will outline the rationale for the process and anticipated benefits at the front end of the workshop? What types of power does this person bring to the process to support its credibility and potential impact?

   - *Focus:* Check to make sure that your client is comfortable with the time and degree of emphasis on each objective. Think about time blocks in relation to the priority of your objectives. Assign a number to each objective and place it next to the agenda block that focuses on that objective. For example, put #2 to represent objective #2 next to each block in the agenda that addresses that objective. Summarize what this says about the design in a discussion with your client.

1

Checklist: Reviewing a Preliminary Design, Cont'd.

Talk about your objectives in terms of percentage of time allotment. Indicate what percentage of your agenda is devoted to each objective. Is this percentage appropriate given its nature, priority, and the pre-work and supportive documentation prepared to support this objective? Is this percentage appropriate when compared to the time allotted to other objectives?

- *Stakeholders:* Review the participant list to ensure that you have a range of perspectives in the room to support an inclusive approach.

How does the design support the group's participation style?

How does participant seating work to support this design?

When should people be seated in homogenous groups? Why?

When should people be seated in heterogeneous groups? Why?

When should you use criteria to organize seating to encourage a maximum mix of perspectives in discussions?

Should people stay in the same groups throughout the entire process? Why? Why not?

- *Core assumptions:* What are the top two assumptions anchoring the process that need to be emphasized at the front end of this design?
- *Key considerations:* What issues will generate the most energy (flash points and fermentation points) in this process? Why?
- *Governance:* Where in the design are those accountable for the success of this initiative given time to support intended outputs and outcomes?
- *Essential documents:* Is anyone likely to be disadvantaged during discussions as a result of not having the same baseline information as others in the group?

2. How does the design accommodate a range of learning and participation styles? What percentage of the design will be focused on:
   - Listening to speakers
   - Hands-on interactive activities such as case studies and problem solving

Checklist: Reviewing a Preliminary Design, Cont'd.

- Small group discussions
- Plenary discussion
- Reflection
- Decision making

Are these percentages appropriate given your objectives and expected outputs and outcomes? Is there enough variety to encourage continuous participation for all involved?

3. What can participants learn that is of value to them and their organizations and is additional to the process objectives?

4. What values anchor how decision making will happen throughout the process? How is this reflected in the design?

5. Every process has a transition point where the focus of participants moves from objectives to outcomes: how does your design enable this transition? What can you say to support this change in focus?

This transition time is a turning point for the design. It often happens after a "storming" phase (Tuckman, 1965) when people have sorted out how the process will evolve and have accepted the need to work together as well as the suggested design and the approach to facilitation. You can trigger it by asking people how the current discussion relates to anticipated outcomes or by commenting on what you notice; for example, "Now that we have confirmed these criteria, we can start to move into the meat of the issues."

This is the point when the facilitator may think, "OK, now we're really starting to move on this agenda. This feels good."

6. What words would you use to describe the pace of this design? Do these words reflect the PTR?

7. What makes this particular process unique? How is this uniqueness reflected in the design?

8. What needs to happen to make this process exceptional?

1

STEP 5. CHECK THE PRELIMINARY DESIGN WITH OTHERS

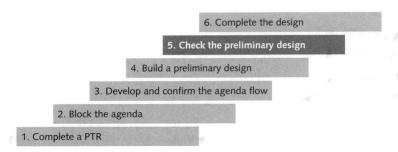

6. Complete the design

5. Check the preliminary design

4. Build a preliminary design

3. Develop and confirm the agenda flow

2. Block the agenda

1. Complete a PTR

Share the draft design with your client and key planning committee members. Ask them to review it and provide feedback. Provide specific questions for their consideration:

* Does the flow make sense based on your understanding of the challenge?

* Are the time allocations appropriate? (Note topics that you think should get more time or less time.)

* Which parts look most interesting to you? Least interesting? Most challenging?

* If you were facilitating this design, what would you see as the low-risk sections? What would you see as the high-risk sections?

Keep the design review group small. For most people involved with a process, this is simply too much information. It's like sharing the smallest technical details of a building plan with people who aren't architects.

Consider sharing your ideas and concerns with another process consultant. Sharing experiences in learning partnerships is a great way to prevent unnecessary interventions and take a design up a notch in terms of excellence.

> Designs rarely permit easy answers to difficult questions, so why do we expect that? And why do we yearn for it even though complexity is the source of our work?

STEP 6. COMPLETE THE DESIGN

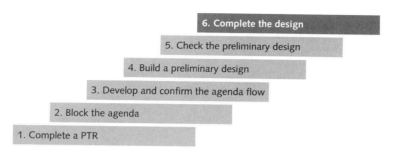

6. Complete the design

5. Check the preliminary design

4. Build a preliminary design

3. Develop and confirm the agenda flow

2. Block the agenda

1. Complete a PTR

This final step is often time-consuming, as it requires considerable attention to detail:

- Insert activities and methods.
- Outline key points for speakers.
- Include reminders about facilitation such as "Take a strategic perspective here, not an operational one," or "Ensure that everyone contributes ideas during this brainstorming session."
- Identify specific questions for group discussions.
- Be specific about timing; for example, remind people to be back from lunch on time.
- Insert seating instructions such as this one: "People return after lunch to the second table number on the back of their name tags."

PROPOSITIONS

1. Processes are dynamic, evolving, and often predictable entities.

2. Process design is intuitive, rational, artistic, scientific, and all of these together.

3. Process design evolves the gray areas of an issue into black-and-white conclusions.

4. When it comes to design, *simple* doesn't mean *easy.*

2 Guidelines for Process Design

This chapter focuses on seven guidelines that make process designs dynamic, relevant, engaging, and productive:

- Make upstream prevention a priority.
- Curb the "overs."
- Think strategically about expertise.
- Listen for mental maps.
- Approach time consciously.
- Create an environment that supports learning.
- Rethink openings and closings.

MAKE UPSTREAM PREVENTION A PRIORITY

Great process designs focus on prevention. By spending time up front to explore and understand a situation, you can create a design that helps prevent the need for rescue interventions later on that distract a group from its real work: achieving its purpose and objectives.

The "upstream prevention" metaphor comes from a parable about a successful small village located in a beautiful valley near a clear rushing stream (Figure 2.1). When the enchanting foothills surrounding the village were declared a park, visitors came to the edge of the hills to watch the stream cascading over rocks and down into the valley. One day someone slipped and fell into the stream, and the

29

villagers rescued him and called the park warden to take care of his injuries. This distracted the villagers from fishing and farming, which were the basis of their economy and an important part of their daily lives.

People continued to fall into the river and the villagers continued to rescue them and call for ambulances to treat their injuries. After several rescues a couple of people in the village climbed to the top of the hill and noticed that it was crumbling from too much foot traffic. They persuaded the park warden to put up a sign where the ground was firm and safe. The sign said "Caution: Extreme Danger Beyond This Sign. Unsafe Ground." The sign prevented many people from falling into the stream, but it didn't stop them all.

So the villagers intervened again. They persuaded the park warden to erect a fence from which people could see the stream and yet not fall in. They also worked with the warden to create a safe path partway down the side of the hill that more adventurous people could take if they wanted to see the stream up close without fear of falling onto the rocks below.

As a result of the villagers' thinking upstream, very few people fell into the water. Occasionally someone would take a risk and have to be rescued, but this happened infrequently. The villagers' fishing and farming were largely uninterrupted.

When upstream prevention is top of mind in process design, you are focused on what you can do early in a project to avoid potential pitfalls and make it the best experience possible. For example:

- By understanding the context and history of a process, you can avoid repeating what hasn't worked in the past and focus on supporting what is more likely to work in the present.

- By coming to agreement on the potential benefits and challenges to key stakeholders and who should be involved in what parts of a process, you can avoid overlooking individuals, groups, and organizations who could make a significant contribution to the purpose of the process. You can also avoid alienating stakeholders who need to be on board to implement decisions resulting from the process.

- By taking enough time—usually several iterations—to ensure that the purpose and objectives of a process are clear and concise and acceptable to all stakeholders, you can prevent revisiting them unnecessarily in the middle of a process.

Downstream Intervention   **Upstream Prevention**

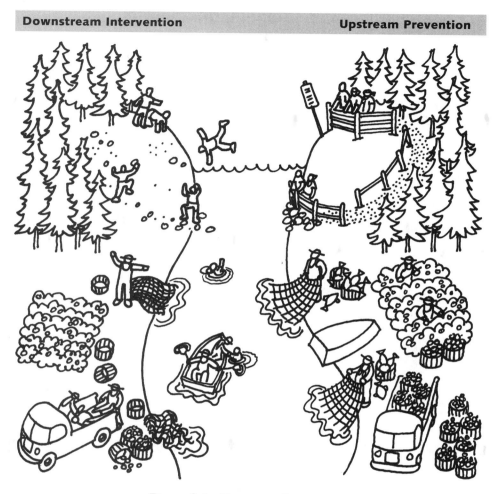

Figure 2.1. Upstream Prevention

- By engaging people who have a range of views, you can uncover perspectives that might be missed in other situations.

- By supporting transparency among stakeholders regarding key assumptions and core considerations for an initiative, you can enable candid and informed discussions able to support healthy and productive interpersonal relationships.

- By ensuring that those involved have the information required to support discussion and decision making throughout a process, you can support a level playing field with respect to who has what information and enable development of the best decisions possible.

The idea is not to try to prevent all interventions: they are a normal and predictable part of a facilitator's role. The idea is to prevent unnecessary interventions that may require treatment downstream that could prove costly in terms of outputs and outcomes.

The following measures are useful in preventing downstream interventions:

- Estimate each activity's level of risk.

- Customize designs to meet customer specifications.

- Be concrete and specific about levels of abstraction.

- Trust the process—but "tie your camel."

> When we have had a clear focus on prevention in designing a process, we enter the facilitation part with a strong sense of confidence about the outcomes. It feels good to know that we have explored most contingencies and have some ideas about how to handle them.

Estimate Risk

Avoid assigning challenging tasks prematurely. In most designs a general rule is to put lower-risk activities earlier in the agenda and higher-risk activities later on when people have had an opportunity to implement some norms for working together. The degree of risk is assessed from the participants' perspective.

Customize Designs

Regardless of what you see advertised, there is no single approach, tool, or type of process that works best in most situations. If only design and facilitation were that simple!

If you take on a single method or approach as the best way to design and facilitate a process before you have done the work to develop a PTR, then you are starting with an assumption that your value proposition is the one that works best for clients rather than starting with the situation and asking, "What would work best here?" When you begin with a PTR, your starting point is active inquiry about a situation, not an answer or approach, regardless of how comfortable you are with that approach or method, or how many times you have seen it work well.

> Processes and their attendant situations are always more complex than the ideas we use to understand them.

Just as you never step into the same river twice because it is constantly flowing, so process consultants never step into the same situation twice because every situation is constantly evolving. We may recognize the shoreline and some trees and shrubs and other topography from past visits to the river, but the water, the energy, the undertows, the wave pattern, and the fish and other creatures are always in flux.

Give the lie to the adage that "once a consultant has a hammer, every situation becomes a nail." Instead, bring fresh eyes to each situation: start with an inquiring mind and a willingness to explore what is unique.

Be Concrete and Specific

Saying "Let's agree on five specific behaviors that will help us work together well throughout this process" is more productive than saying "We need to work together well to make this process a success." The more concrete and specific you are about what everyone needs to do, the more success you are likely to experience in the design.

> A client in state B who had seen a national consensus-building process work in state A was adamant that it would also work well in state B. However, the population demographics, political structure, and climate in state A was much more resistant to change than in state B. After this information was presented in a discussion paper, the committee supported state B in taking a less comprehensive approach to the process than was required in state A, saving approximately $150,000, which was retargeted to implementation costs.

It is also helpful to be concrete in how you name things. In technical environments, use the appropriate technical language to avoid confusion about what you mean. If a process about cleaning up effluent from a manufacturing plant is described as being about environmental corporate social responsibility, then the language doesn't accurately represent the purpose of the process. The objectives are being hidden in a destructive form of euphemism: language that cloaks intent.

Both the designer and the facilitator can support an appropriate level of abstraction in a process. For example, you may start discussions about an issue at a relatively high level of abstraction to find an area of agreement as a starting point for discussion. Then you can work the design to more specific issues once that agreement is in place—allowing the discussion to flow from the general to the specific.

Be concrete with speakers about the specific level of abstraction that the design requires for success. Higher levels can be so abstract as to preclude discussions focused on the concrete realities of participants. Encourage speakers to give specific examples for abstract statements. Inform each speaker about what participants will be doing before and after their presentations, and be clear about your expectation that they will refer to work prior to their presentation and help prepare participants to discuss questions after their presentation.

Avoid or address situations in a design where a speaker or participant gives too much power to a single example based on an abstraction. For example, you may see an advertisement asking you to donate to a clean water initiative in a low-resource country in Africa. This is a fairly abstract idea—but then the picture under the request is of thin, starving children looking abandoned and very ill. The picture or example that takes the level of abstraction lower has too much power because not all children in poor African countries look like this: it's a stereotyped cliché that doesn't necessarily benefit the popular perspective of those countries.

The use of PowerPoint is another example: it makes it too easy to turn presentations into vague verbal maps about what is in reality complicated territory and subject matter. Check PowerPoint presentations prior to a session to ensure that the level of abstraction is appropriate for your anticipated outcomes. Make sure they are not so sketchy that the important evidence (such as the flaw that could destroy the spaceship) is omitted.

Trust the Process?

We like to say, "Trust the process—but tie your camel!" This revision of the old Sufi saying "Trust in Allah but tie your camel" reflects the reality behind a common maxim of process consulting: "Things may get a little rough but you have to learn to trust the process—it will all work out the way it's meant to be." However, just as the Sufi saying points out that you'd better have a backup plan to prevent your camel from slipping away, so process consultants need to "tie their camels" in many ways to prevent a process from slipping away.

Whether you are an internal or external process consultant, in your hometown or another country, working in a single culture and language or with multiple cultures and languages, one of the best ways to ensure your camel is secure is to know enough about the content involved that you can feel confident facilitating experts in that area. This requires a commitment to doing some research, learning common acronyms, and understanding key terms so that you don't hold up discussions by asking what something means when group members are already resonating on a shared wavelength.

Another way to tie your camel is to identify points where you think the process is more vulnerable and could go off the rails. If you're prepared when this happens and have some options in mind for how to intervene, you will probably feel fairly confident that your camel won't get away.

And although it may sound trite, through experience, education, expertise, training, and perspectives, process consultants develop a fairly sophisticated intuitive sense about whether they need to think about ways to secure a current process further than what is already in place. Trust your gut.

CURB THE "OVERS"

Avoid overprocessing, overconsulting, overexplaining, overinforming, over-questioning, overmeeting, over- anything.

- If you are supposed to be working at a strategic level, avoid operational approaches.

- If you are supposed to be doing an initial consultation, avoid questions that take you in depth on an issue.

- If you are supposed to be providing information that will help you address a specific aspect of an issue, avoid providing so much information that it takes you down roads you don't need to explore.

- Avoid overprocessing. How many questions are you using to get stakeholders' opinions on a topic?

- Avoid overconsulting. Too many surveys, opinion polls, interviews, or market research sessions can make respondents feel that you are avoiding decision making.

- Avoid overmeeting. Too many meetings with clients build insecurity rather than confidence. Too many sessions with planning committees are perceived to be annoying rather than inclusive.

- Avoid overfacilitating. Saul Alinsky (a community development activist) advised people not to do anything for anyone else that they could do for themselves. This is a wise approach to design. Actively look for opportunities for participants to do for themselves what you are tempted to do for them—everything from developing a PTR to designing small group discussions. This approach to facilitative leadership enables group members to act in the best interests of the group and own the results of their decisions.

THINK STRATEGICALLY ABOUT EXPERTISE

Where is the best expertise you can find to support your process?

If the most competent experts are participants in the meetings and workshops, design the agenda to get the most out of them in relation to your objectives. Tell participants that they are the people who are most informed on this topic and you have set up the agenda to bring what they know to the forefront in discussions and decision-making efforts. Avoid bringing in speakers who may not have as much experience or expertise as the participants.

If the best expertise is found in the literature on your subject, prepare an easily accessible and specific document that summarizes what the literature says in relation to your objectives, outputs, and outcomes. Then have that document reviewed by a credible panel prior to printing it (in draft form) and use it throughout your agenda as your main reference document. By presenting it clea "working draft," you can ask participants for suggestions for a final versi thus avoid having the document itself become an issue throughout the pro

If you can only find experts to address specific subtopics and no one to address an area as a whole, design your agenda to accommodate a topic that can be broken down into panel presentations or create a collaborative writing initiative to develop a background document.

LISTEN FOR MENTAL MAPS

Process consultants, clients, stakeholders, and participants bring a multitude of mental maps to any initiative. Some may be based on their personal experiences in similar situations—these can be seen as maps (or models) *of the world*. Some may be based on their beliefs of how things ought to be—these can be seen as maps or models *for the world*. Others may be based on what they have heard about from others or learned through reading; they may or may not accurately represent the situation at hand.

The implication for process consultants is to listen very carefully to clients' and stakeholders' views, that is, their maps of the world, or for the world, or both. Process consultants will need to be able to facilitate their way through and around these verbal maps in the process of creating a design.

APPROACH TIME CONSCIOUSLY

Time is a fundamental building block in process design. It's also an influential factor in how successful people are when working in groups.

Do you recognize any of the following?

- Clients say they can spare a day or half a day to do a process that you know requires a minimum of two days.

- Preparation time to support effective process work is undervalued, and some clients are willing to pay for only a fraction of your usual preparation time.

2

- Harried committee members complain about not having enough time to do what needs to be done to support a process.

- Deadlines are used deliberately to keep people moving, and without immediate pressure to produce, many people feel guilty about their roles on a committee.

- You are challenged to make sure that participants in a process work more efficiently and do more in less time.

Given frequent pressures to compress time in interactive processes, it is useful for process consultants to see themselves as guardians of time. Clients may not know what can be accomplished in a specific time period. Depending on the context, you may find yourself saying things like these:

"When you think about the cost of bringing all these people together to do this work, I think we could be a little more ambitious about what we could get done. How about if we add another objective related to team development?"

"We only have one day for this session, and you have already booked the morning solid with invited speakers. That leaves us two blocks of an hour and a half each in the afternoon to meet all the other objectives. Let's take a close look at what can be accomplished in that time period."

The time allotted to doing a task can be quite different from the time it takes to complete a task in a session. What is your inclination? Do you tend to allow adequate time, less time, or more time than it takes for participants to accomplish a task?

Time lines for completing tasks are often unrealistic given the contingencies of working environments. Managers in a process may want the work done quickly, while those doing the work may want to focus more on doing it well. The two are not always compatible.

Check in with your client and planning committee members to get their perspectives on how much time is required for a task in a design. When less time is allotted than it takes to do a task, or when a client expects task completion no matter how short the time span available, it is often the last part of a process that suffers, that is, time for feedback and closure or for monitoring outcomes.

Firmness and Flexibility

Be both firm and flexible when it comes to timing. Stand firm regarding how much time it takes to do something well. Be flexible when it comes to adjusting purpose and objectives to match the time available or when a group working on a task needs more time to get its work done. In most processes, people need clear and reasonable time lines about both clock time and what kind of method to use for a given period (for example, brainstorming, prioritizing)—otherwise their work tends to expand to fit whatever time is available. Some process consultants keep a log of what can be done within certain time frames so that they have data at their fingertips to support discussions and decision making about timing.

When developing an agenda, time concerns often emerge as, "We have to have these five speakers at the front end of our agenda. But if we have them all, it will severely limit our time for dialogue and decision making. How can we do both well?" Use a blocked agenda to make the point about the time available and required to do a good job on specific outcomes. Point to the time blocks where each objective is being addressed. The value of speakers in interactive processes can be overestimated. A group may well include its own experts, who know as much—or more—about the specific implications of an issue than an expert brought in from outside.

Be Deliberate About Airtime

The time during which someone is speaking is commonly called *airtime*. Some people may learn or think by talking with others and therefore can consume a lot of airtime; others may prefer to reflect silently or to listen to others, and thus their opinions and suggestions may not be voiced.

The amount of individual airtime in a design can have a significant impact on the final product and how others feel about it. Several factors influence how much airtime individuals use in processes, for example:

- How verbally enthusiastic and creative they are
- How perceptive and skilled other group members and the facilitator are when intervening to support equitable participation
- How much expertise, experience, and authority individuals have in the group

2

Do the math. If a group of eight people has twenty minutes to do a task and the group facilitator needs two minutes to explain the task and intervene occasionally, then each person would have less than two minutes to talk. Is this the right amount of time to do this task well?

Be strategic about airtime when developing a design. Do you want participants to experience some time pressure to encourage creativity, or do you prefer to have more time for critical reflection? Sometimes it's important for the facilitator to support the design by explaining how much airtime each person has for a task: "In this kind of work the task often expands to fill the time available. The time we have for this task is twenty minutes. You may feel a little rushed doing this brainstorming activity, but given that the best ideas often come up first, especially when there is some pressure, it's a conscious decision to take this approach."

CREATE AN ENVIRONMENT THAT SUPPORTS LEARNING

When people get together to do things such as issues analysis, strategic planning, organizational change, training and development, significant opportunities for individual and organizational learning are present (Senge, 1990, paraphrased from pp. 6–11).

> At its essence, every organization is a product of how its members think and interact. . . . Changing the way we interact means redesigning not just the formal structures of the organization, but the hard-to-see patterns of interaction between people and processes. . . . Learning in organizations means the continuous testing of experience, and the transformation of that experience into knowledge—accessible to the whole organization, and relevant to its core purpose.
>
> —Peter Senge and others, 1994, pp. 48-49.

Great process designs integrate the principles of adult learning throughout their implementation.

How do the designs you develop enable participants to learn from one another? In Figure 2.2, circle a number on the accompanying scale to indicate the extent to which you incorporate basic adult learning principles in your process designs.

40

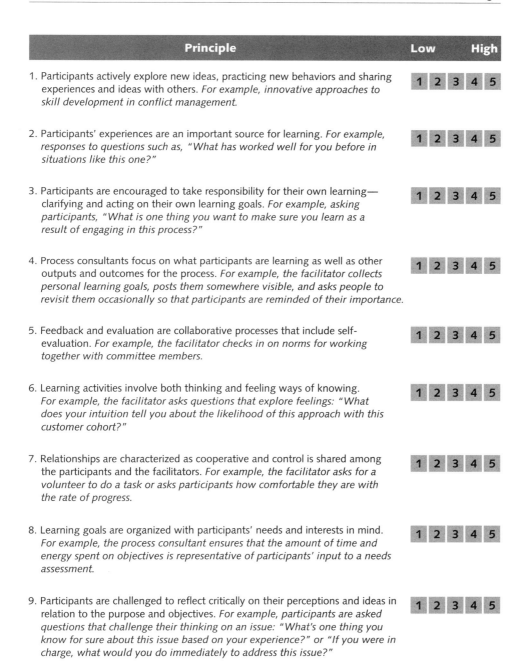

Principle	Low				High
1. Participants actively explore new ideas, practicing new behaviors and sharing experiences and ideas with others. *For example, innovative approaches to skill development in conflict management.*	1	2	3	4	5
2. Participants' experiences are an important source for learning. *For example, responses to questions such as, "What has worked well for you before in situations like this one?"*	1	2	3	4	5
3. Participants are encouraged to take responsibility for their own learning—clarifying and acting on their own learning goals. *For example, asking participants, "What is one thing you want to make sure you learn as a result of engaging in this process?"*	1	2	3	4	5
4. Process consultants focus on what participants are learning as well as other outputs and outcomes for the process. *For example, the facilitator collects personal learning goals, posts them somewhere visible, and asks people to revisit them occasionally so that participants are reminded of their importance.*	1	2	3	4	5
5. Feedback and evaluation are collaborative processes that include self-evaluation. *For example, the facilitator checks in on norms for working together with committee members.*	1	2	3	4	5
6. Learning activities involve both thinking and feeling ways of knowing. *For example, the facilitator asks questions that explore feelings: "What does your intuition tell you about the likelihood of this approach with this customer cohort?"*	1	2	3	4	5
7. Relationships are characterized as cooperative and control is shared among the participants and the facilitators. *For example, the facilitator asks for a volunteer to do a task or asks participants how comfortable they are with the rate of progress.*	1	2	3	4	5
8. Learning goals are organized with participants' needs and interests in mind. *For example, the process consultant ensures that the amount of time and energy spent on objectives is representative of participants' input to a needs assessment.*	1	2	3	4	5
9. Participants are challenged to reflect critically on their perceptions and ideas in relation to the purpose and objectives. *For example, participants are asked questions that challenge their thinking on an issue: "What's one thing you know for sure about this issue based on your experience?" or "If you were in charge, what would you do immediately to address this issue?"*	1	2	3	4	5

Figure 2.2. Adult Learning Principles

RETHINK OPENINGS AND CLOSINGS

Workshop openings usually get significant consideration by process consultants. Not so with workshop endings, which often end up being opportunities for catch-up time. How often have you thought or heard, "We're a little behind right now but we can make it up by shortening the closing."

Openings and closings are equally important because they book-end a design. As a result, they both play essential roles in developing ownership, building a climate for supporting change, and attending to the process needs of participants. They also connect the stages of a multiphase process.

When selecting people to participate in openings and closings, consider who is in a position to support the design outcomes: do you need someone with positional power, influence power, implementation power, or perhaps someone who was an early resister? (See Chapter 4.)

Consider identifying three participants to do short closing remarks, say about two minutes each. Choose people who bring different perspectives: one person could represent a large organization, another a small organization; one person could have a research orientation, another that of the government. Each person could respond to two questions in their closing remarks. For example:

- What is one thing that stood out for you at this meeting?
- What message will you be taking back to your team or organization?

Ensure that your closing reflects and furthers the purpose of the workshop: if the workshop is about team development, then have a closing piece that boosts team development rather than (or in addition to) someone talking about what needs to happen next.

AND FINALLY . . .

Regardless of how careful you are when developing a design and related questions or how much expertise you have in a field, keep in mind that the best insights often come from experiencing what happens when a design stalls or a question doesn't work exactly the way you expected. As with most things in life, you need to create designs several times to really feel comfortable with the tension inherent in collaborative, consensus-building processes with uncertain outcomes.

PROPOSITIONS

5. Effective process design requires a prevention perspective.

6. Effective process consultants (as designers and facilitators) can fit comfortably in a broad range of environments without ever sacrificing their essence.

7. The process populates the design.

8. The client is always part of the problem. The client may not always know best.

9. Don't just expect the unexpected: prepare for it.

2

2 THE PEOPLE FACTORS: PERSPECTIVES, POWER, AND VALUES

Process design is about working collaboratively with others. This requires a comprehensive understanding of people's perspectives, the risks and benefits of the various types of power they bring to a process, and the nature of values tensions inherent in different points of view.

Chapter Three explores ways to include a range of views in understanding a situation. It provides practical guidelines for taking a comprehensive and integrative approach to both individual and group perspectives.

Chapter Four describes how to work constructively with the various types of power that people bring to a process. Naming and capitalizing on individual and group power enriches the potential of a process design, particularly in terms of support for change.

Chapter Five begins with a focus on understanding and integrating values in process design. It then presents a values hierarchy as a tool to support skills in listening for and understanding values.

3 The Perspectives Factor in Process Design

Process designs that work engage people with different perspectives in exploring similarities and differences and then searching for solutions that go beyond their own individual visions of what is possible. This comprehensive, integrative approach is essential to ensuring that a process design is practical, realistic, and complete.

A *comprehensive approach* is an inclusive one: it takes a range of perspectives into consideration with respect to the purpose and objectives of a process and the factors surrounding it. This may include commissioning a thorough review of the literature and documenting the history leading up to a process. It may involve stakeholders as committee members, as participants in key meetings and workshops, and in consultations, phone interviews, surveys, and questionnaires. Or it may just involve interviews with three leading individuals who can contribute different perspectives.

An *integrative approach* brings together key elements into a larger whole. "Integrative thinking is a cross-functional approach to problem solving that views often-imperceptible features as significant to resolution; considers complex cause-and-effect relationships; keeps the 'big picture' in mind, while concentrating on all the elements individually; and refuses to accept trade-offs in the problem's resolution, turning obstacles into opportunities" (Martin, n.d., p. 2).

Facilitated processes come in many degrees of complexity. They often engage participants in challenging, unstable, and ambiguous issues where robust choices are required to guide future action. An integrative approach that begins with a comprehensive understanding of a situation can support planners in attending to

> Meaning is all we want.
> Choices are all we make.
> Relationships are all we have.
> —Schuman, 2006, p. xxiii

a broad range of factors and perspectives while developing creative options and keeping their eyes on their objectives.

Information from various perspectives helps clarify the purpose and objectives of an initiative. Figure 3.1 illustrates this: when you have one perspective on a situation, things look very different from the complete picture you get based on a comprehensive, integrative approach.

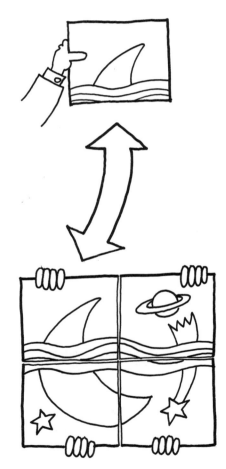

Figure 3.1. **Perspectives in Process Design**

One participant in a process may have a potentially intimidating image about the challenge at hand. However, when you bring other participants to the table, their joint perspectives can present a more complete and constructive image.

MINING PERSPECTIVES

Here are suggestions for how to explore client and stakeholder perspectives:

- Differentiate and clarify client perspectives.
- Support a collaborative approach.
- Identify and move beyond the presenting issue.
- Clarify and name stakeholder perspectives.
- Be familiar with your clients' and stakeholders' language.

Differentiate and Clarify Client Perspectives

A process usually involves several clients, each with their own interests and expectations:

- *Contact* clients make the initial approach to the internal manager or external consultant.
- *Primary* clients own a problem for which they want assistance and have decision-making authority.
- *Intermediate* clients get involved in early meetings or planning next steps.
- *Ultimate* clients may or may not be directly involved with the consultant or manager, but their welfare, interest, and stake in the project must be considered (Schein, 1987, pp. 117–18, adapted).

In addition, certain clients are more active in process design and facilitation during certain parts of a process, and it is not unusual to have both the client and consultant agree to shift from one role to another during a process. For example, you may decide partway through a process that an ultimate client should facilitate part of the process rather than function as a full participant.

3

A *contact client* makes the initial approach to the consultant (internal or external), and this is likely to be the point where you will get your first impression of the situation. Use this first contact to determine whether this work is within your area of expertise and your current schedule.

Sometimes a contact client will decline to provide any information other than naming the presenting issue and will instead refer you to a *primary client* who owns the problem, has decision-making authority, and to whom you would be accountable if you took on the work. If this is the case, be prepared to ask the primary client specific questions to help you understand the problem. These questions might explore why you have been contacted, the relationship between the contact client and other clients, when the decision was made to get a process consultant involved, efforts to date to address the issue, and the relative urgency of the situation. As a process consultant, you are accountable to your primary client while keeping in mind your responsibilities to other clients in an initiative.

Avoid taking on a primary client's problem as if it were your own. Maintaining clear boundaries about who owns a problem is an essential skill in both process design and facilitation. These boundaries prevent overdependence in problem solving when the consultant (internal or external) and the client need each other in order to feel whole. Overdependence may arise for several reasons: personal insecurities, potential financial benefit, personal promotion, feeling comfortable with one another, or not having the energy to explore new options. Whatever the reason, the result can jeopardize outcomes and may evolve into unethical behavior.

Intermediate clients get involved after you have confirmed that you will take on the work. They are often committee members, important stakeholders, and others who have a vested interest in how the process is developed and managed. Intermediate clients have the potential for significant impact on how a process moves forward, and also in decision making and post-process implementation.

Ultimate clients may or may not be directly involved with a process consultant, but their welfare, interest, and stake in the project must be protected. In the public sector and in civil society, the ultimate client often has more at stake than the primary client. For example, a government department may hire you as a process consultant to support policy development related to access to public transportation for people with disabilities—the latter are your ultimate clients even though you may not be directly involved with them.

Different types of clients have priority at different times during a process. Often more than one client will have top priority. For example, you may need to keep both your primary client and ultimate clients as top priority with respect to accountability for outcomes: the primary client may have decision-making authority, while the ultimate client may have more influence with stakeholders.

> Ambiguity about who is what type of client is common. Clarify roles and responsibilities as soon as possible and in writing to prevent confusion.

Support a Collaborative Approach

Stakeholders and clients bring a range of perspectives to an initiative. Collaboration forges these perspectives into a shared, integrative, and comprehensive understanding of what is required for a successful process. It is people working together that generates solutions that work, no matter what the scope of the process.

Clarify up front what collaboration means to those involved in a process. Explore what each person brings to the table, how they see their roles, what each expects to achieve, and the implications of their presence at the table. Set norms for working together—particularly with respect to how decisions will be made.

Identify and Move Beyond the Presenting Issue

When contact clients describe why they are requesting your services, you are often hearing about the *presenting issue*—an initial understanding or perspective on a problem. The presenting issue is not necessarily the real issue: it is simply an initial perspective and may focus more on symptoms than on the real problem.

> Collaborative tensility is the ability of collaborative partners to bend and remain flexible under pressure so that their work can maintain momentum despite challenges.
> —Schuman, 2006, p. 470

As you consult with clients and stakeholders to get more perspective, the presenting issue usually starts to blossom into a more realistic understanding of a problematic situation.

Clarify and Name Stakeholder Perspectives

Stakeholders may wear several hats: they can be leaders, managers, sources of information, change agents, experts, and researchers, to mention a few. Each of these perspectives is important in gaining a full understanding of a situation.

> I am not struck so much by the diversity of testimony as by the many-sidedness of truth.
> —Baldwin, 1989, p. 95

By naming stakeholder perspectives you can identify which stakeholders bring those perspectives to the table. Ultimately, when it comes to the relationship between participants and outcomes, it's "quality participants in—quality products out."

> The more we come into a situation as open-minded investigators, the happier we are with the intelligence we can gather to support next steps. In addition to identifying formal roles, we also see everyone who has a stake in the success of the initiative as a potential change agent.

Be Familiar with Your Clients' and Stakeholders' Language

Perspectives are intertwined with language, the #1 tool in process design and facilitation. As a result, the words you use can make a big difference to the tone and productivity of a process. Learn and use language that reflects the realities of your clients and stakeholders. Some useful questions to ask yourself:

- How do these clients use specific words in this initiative? Consider words such as *strategic, goal, objective, issue, customer, client,* and *consumer.* Is there a lexicon available (or can you develop one) for this subject area that all stakeholders would agree to use?

- What words might be politically incorrect—that is, function as lightning rods in this situation? Why?

> Because words are used in a specific context, "no word ever has the same meaning twice."
> —Hayakawa, 1990 (1939), p. 39

3

- What are new and emerging words and phrases in this field?
- What are the most common acronyms? Which (if any) can get confused?

GROUP PARTICIPATION STYLES

Much has been written about individual styles and preferences as documented in instruments such as learning style inventories, personality assessments, leadership styles, and so on. In a similar vein, many groups have process participation styles that reflect participants' accumulated life experience, job training, and perspectives of the world.

Process designers and facilitators often comment on these participation styles or temperaments:

"We work with court judges a lot, and they're a bright group and tend to be strongly opinionated. We have become accustomed to how they think, what they like to do in a process, and what it takes to build consensus. They really enjoy arguing things through so we need to make sure there is enough time for that."

"This group was primarily experienced bureaucrats. They understood all the practical implications of new policy in this area and took all the time they needed to ensure that their decisions took these implications into consideration. The meeting ended up being far too short for the amount of work involved."

"This group of senior directors was really experienced, and almost anyone there could have done the facilitation. They were energetic and really owned the process and what they needed to do to make it work."

"The senior vice president was very clear before we started: he didn't want to get any action items as a result of the process. Unfortunately, the ten assistant vice-presidents in the company had the same philosophy—so the process was all about passing the buck. Very disappointing. We just couldn't design our way around the apathy and lack of ownership for outcomes at the senior level."

As process consultants in the world of high-performance sport we noticed that athletes, coaches, and leaders who had spent many years focused on a sport frequently exhibited behaviors characteristic of that sport. For example, ex-swimmers

3

who had spent hours every day in a pool going up and down lanes while making small corrections in their strokes could be just as focused and persistent later in their lives in sticking to a task that required small adjustments until it was finished. Swimmers also tended to bring the characteristics of an individual sport competitor to their involvement in process design: they liked to be given a task and then do it rather than discuss it extensively in a group.

The Dangers of Stereotyping

It's dangerous to stretch observations about participation style into a guiding principle. Comments about stereotyping are sure to surface, and justifiably so.

However, as a reflective tool, thinking about group participation styles has been extremely helpful in our work in process design and facilitation. It has helped us to notice group behaviors and characteristics that have an impact on process outcomes. For example, when designing a session for litigation lawyers (who have likely spent many years listening for holes in arguments rather than listening for a way to understand and work with various perspectives), we use a different approach to collaborative consensus building than we would if we were doing strategic planning with an association of psychologists whose work is to listen professionally all day long.

> The key to avoiding stereotyping is to check out every single inference you make about a group's participation style.

Think about your style as a process consultant and which groups you like to work with most. Does your style work better with some groups than with others?

Participation Styles in Decision Making

Consider group participation styles with respect to decision making. (These conclusions do not apply to heterogeneous groups.) For example, if your client group consists of emergency department physicians who make urgent decisions all day long and in very short periods of time, it's probably a good idea to design an efficient and comprehensive decision-making process in which you have clear and strong evidence to support discussion. Other groups may react quite differently:

- Social workers may need more time to explore options and accommodate people's feelings in a group as a prelude to making a decision.

- Public service employees crave efficient decision making in workshops while at the same time understanding that their complex work environment and the nature of public policy can make this a challenge.

- Financial officers who are most comfortable with decisions based on balance sheets may resist other types of decision making unless the new criteria are thoroughly explained.

- Public policy developers will probably require a broad range of expert opinion to help shape decisions on issues.

3

What all this adds up to is not a stereotype but a recognition that certain—although not all—homogenous groups tend to have accumulated experiences that have an impact on design. And if you add the individual personalities of participants to this mix, you have a delightfully complex stew when it comes to understanding a group!

Three Keys to Group Participation Styles

Nuance is important in understanding a group's dominant participation style and then designing and facilitating processes that support a constructive climate for discussion and decision making. Three keys to understanding group participation style are the culture in which participants function, the extent to which they value autonomy, and the type of expertise they bring to the process.

Culture

Culture includes the shared values, norms, traditions, history, institutions, ways of doing things, and perspectives of a group of people.

Pay attention to the various cultures involved in a process when developing designs: working with environmentalists may be quite different from working with corporate directors or bureaucrats. Each area of expertise has its own culture, decision-making processes, hierarchy, and traditions that will have an impact on how individuals participate in a process.

Sample questions for exploring participant cultures:

- What is unique about the culture in which this process is taking place— for example, values related to public participation or to professional authority?

- Overall, does this culture generally welcome change, resist change, or ignore change? What are the implications of this for development of questions—for example, discussion about controversial issues?

- Do experts in this culture generally have a narrow, rather exclusive perspective of issues in their field and who should address them, or do they have a broader, more inclusive perspective?

- To what extent is tradition valued in this group?

- What standards are used for reflecting on quality of work in this field? What are the implications of these standards in relation to question development?

Autonomy

Autonomy is about independence and self-determination. In process design, some groups are more focused on autonomy than others. For example, this is particularly evident when an established profession is concerned about losing ground to technicians in the same field who have lesser education, social status, and income, or when an advocacy group is fighting for equal rights.

In the public, union, and not-for-profit sectors in particular, representatives of professional associations are frequently charged with protecting the interests of their constituencies while also having a fiduciary responsibility to take a broader perspective on issues in their field.

Sample questions for exploring participant autonomy:

- How might issues related to professional independence affect the development of the process?

- Does one group of stakeholders see itself as holding the correct answer?

- Do any stakeholders perceive themselves to be adversaries or in competition with other stakeholders? In what context? To what extent?

- Is there tension over who should control what gets implemented as a result of the conclusions and recommendations?

- Is there a possibility that decision-making processes could result in contests of will?

- How does decision making happen on a day-to-day basis for participants in this group?

- In their day-to-day work, do most stakeholders pride themselves on working in high-risk situations where they are trained to make decisions individually and quickly, based on their expertise? Or are they accustomed to being inclusive, consulting comprehensively, and discussing issues extensively?

Expertise

The word *expert* means different things in different settings. In some professional cultures it is about citations in peer-reviewed publications. In others it is based on field experience or on age-related wisdom. It is essential for process consultants to understand and appreciate the range and type of expertise engaged in a process and the implications when collaborating with experts on a particular challenge.

Sample questions for exploring participant expertise:

- How do you define expertise?

- Who has the most knowledge or skill in relation to specific areas?

- Do consumers and advocates need to be at the table to contribute their expertise and ensure grassroots support for implementation?

- Where is credibility vested in the area under discussion—for example, in academics at universities, in activists, in rock musicians, in parents, in politicians?

- Where is positional authority vested in the area under discussion—for example, in academia, governments, professional societies, advocacy groups, charities, specialists?

- How do ethical challenges interface with expertise and evidence in the issue under discussion?

Knowing about the factors of autonomy, culture, and expertise (ACE) in a group can stimulate inferences and questions that when reviewed can provide insightful support to the design process.

PROPOSITIONS

10. The presence of divergent perspectives in a process discourages the herd impulse.

11. Groups and organizations have precious few truly visionary thinkers (those who think differently). Address situations that alienate individuals who think differently.

12. The unexamined inference is not worth sharing.

4

The Power Factor
in Process Design

In process terms, *power* is the ability to decide what will happen, the capacity to act, or the ability to get things done. Identifying stakeholders' powers and using them constructively in a process is an important facilitative leadership skill.

Eight types of power are associated with processes that work: positional, personal, reward, coercive, enabling, expert, resource, and relationship (Tomlinson and Strachan, 1996; Cuming, 1981; Kitzmiller, 1991). Each type of power has inherent benefits and risks that must be considered carefully in the context of an initiative. When you can name what type of power you need to develop and implement a process successfully, and who can bring that type of power to your process, your chances of supporting action on outcomes increase considerably.

Consider this scenario: You have designed and facilitated a workshop that has gone very well, resulting in a perceptive report and astute recommendations. Feedback on the flow of the agenda and the facilitation was positive, and people left feeling good about what happened and their roles in contributing to its success. However, you feel uneasy knowing that although your client had the best intentions, the people with the power and commitment to facilitate change after the workshop were not engaged appropriately. And it may not be possible to engage them meaningfully now that the workshop is over.

This means that your apparently successful workshop is just that—a single one-off session in which people appreciated and enjoyed the opportunity to take part, but which at some level both you and the participants know will not go anywhere. The report is likely to sit on the shelf, and nothing will get done.

In our culture of accountability, it is not enough to be an excellent facilitator who gets great feedback on workshop evaluations. Process consultants must ensure that the right people with the right kinds of power and commitment are engaged to implement a design throughout *all* its phases.

Processes happen in a context. That context includes people with the capacity to use power positively to support projected outcomes. The role of a process consultant is to understand and appreciate that context in its fullest sense so as to enable meaningful participation by those with the power and commitment to support expected shorter- and longer-term outcomes.

TYPES OF POWER

For each of the eight types of power described in this chapter, ask yourself:

- Do we need this type of power to support our purpose and objectives? If so, who could bring that type of power to this initiative?

- What other types of power could this person contribute to our success?

- What are the risks and benefits of having this person's potential power at our table? (See accompanying figures, 4.1–4.8.)

Positional Power

Positional power is based on the authority, rights, and privileges of a particular office or job as legitimized by a specific organization or influential sponsor. Positional power can also come from age, experience, gender, or social class. The com-

pliance of others is expected and based on the authority invested in the role or roles the stakeholder fulfills through that position.

Individuals and groups with positional power may include a planning committee chair, a senior executive or president of a corporation, a published scientist with peer credibility, a professor, an activist, a respected leader with influence in an affected community, formal representatives of groups such as a union, a professional association, a board of directors, or appointed or elected officials. Positions may range from those specified by formal job descriptions to those informally agreed upon by small, loosely structured groups.

Examples of potential benefits accrued by engaging people with positional power

- Authorizing the use of facilities and equipment
- Enabling organization-wide support
- Authorizing the provision of resources such as skilled individuals, funding, and use of space and equipment

Examples of potential risks associated with the misuse of positional power

- Overreliance on an individual Steering Committee member in providing advice during a collaborative design process
- Overdependence on an established authority when one outcome is the development of an equitable partnership

---

Figure 4.1. Positional Power—Risks and Benefits

Personal Power

Personal power is functioning when the capacity to act and influence others is the result of influence that people don't usually think of as power. Others may respect someone's manner and way of thinking and acting or see that person as someone whom they can emulate, someone whose judgment they can trust.

For example, participants in a process may buy a book recommended by someone with personal power whose opinion they respect. Such individuals have personal power because people accept their influence without feeling manipulated. Personal power is sometimes called charisma, and its exact source can be a mystery.

Examples of potential benefits accrued by engaging people with personal power

- Contagious enthusiasm about a design for an initiative
- Positive role modeling
- Strong communication of values
- Constructive influencing
- Commitment to a positive outcome that motivates others
- Generation of trusting relationships

Examples of potential risks associated with the misuse of personal power

- Disproportionate influence (often well motivated) by an individual with a specific perspective
- Reduced critical reflection
- Little consideration of a range of options
- Selectivity in the development of supportive information
- Lack of consultation with experts
- Groupthink, particularly when people with considerable personal power are nudging the discussion toward agreement

---

Figure 4.2. Personal Power—Risks and Benefits

Reward Power

Reward power is the capacity to act and influence others based on the ability to provide something that others want or value.

These rewards may be material or emotional. In the carrot-and-stick analogy, reward power is the carrot. Examples include selection to a special team, a promotion, a smile or nod of approval, positive verbal feedback, or a cash prize.

Examples of potential benefits accrued by engaging people with reward power	Examples of potential risks associated with the misuse of reward power
• Opportunities to recognize and reward stakeholders who have made significant contributions	• Perception that appropriate behavior is not valued in itself but rather for a reward
• Support for a constructive working environment based on appreciation of others	• Development of assumed behavior and reward relationships that stifle innovation and creativity
• Team development through a prize such as a piece of sculpture or a wall plaque that everyone on a steering committee receives in recognition of joint efforts	• Awareness that a certain person or group has most of the power of reward and can give or withhold rewards at will

Figure 4.3. Reward Power—Risks and Benefits

Coercive Power

Coercive power is the capacity to act and influence others based on the ability to force others who have little or no possibility of escaping the influence. In the carrot-and-stick analogy, coercive power is the stick.

Coercive power can take many forms—informing middle managers that they must attend and participate fully in a session, telling staff that participation in all aspects of performance feedback is mandatory, letting board members know that those who don't fulfill their fiduciary obligations may not be reappointed. Contrary to first impressions, coercive power can have many positive results, particularly with respect to compliance with standards.

Coercive power may also be used in a less direct manner such as through inducing guilt through the withdrawal of smiles and approval. It can also be associated with factors such as credentials, an outstanding record, wealth, or an important position.

Examples of potential benefits accrued by engaging people with coercive power

- Mandatory involvement of a complete cohort in a process when this is required to support success, as in a consultation or a research initiative
- Compliance with legal require- ments or regulatory frameworks

Examples of potential risks associated with the misuse of coercive power

- Loss of candor in group discussions
- Development of a push-back, obstructive culture in response to excessive control

Figure 4.4. Coercive Power—Risks and Benefits

Enabling Power

Enabling power is the capacity to influence others based on an ability to facilitate them in making choices. In process consulting these choices are often related to purpose, mission, and goals. Enabling power is associated with building an atmos- phere of mutual trust and encouraging individual develop- ment. It also involves the use of appropriate positive and critical feedback in working with others and celebrating people's accomplishments.

Examples include active listening, involving others in plan- ning, supporting the development of mutually beneficial rela- tionships among stakeholders, facilitating appropriate decision making, supporting educational experiences focused on individual and group development.

Examples of potential benefits accrued by engaging people with enabling power	Examples of potential risks associated with the misuse of enabling power
• Participants work together to support their learning objectives and thus achieve more than what they thought was possible	• Overprocessing, resulting in frustration, unwarranted delays, not enough decision making, and missed deadlines
• A committee chair facilitates a group in addressing a conflict successfully	• Oversupport, resulting in individuals and groups not maximizing their potential to address their own issues
• A facilitator increases ownership in a process by involving team members in establishing a workshop agenda	• Unclear boundaries and insufficient ownership and confidence on the part of stakeholders to complete an initiative without assistance from the consultant
• A process consultant builds commitment to outcomes through the development of a PTR	

Figure 4.5. Enabling Power—Risks and Benefits

Expert Power

Expert power is the capacity to act and influence others. It is based on expertise and information (or access to information) in a specific area and the holder's ability to communicate that expertise or information. Others defer to this expertise and depend on it to do their work, solve problems, and address issues.

Individuals with expert power may specialize in a particular area such as rules, strategy, scientific know-how, management skills in operationalizing strategic plans, ethics, or skill development as it relates to a topic being discussed. Although expert power is usually associated with formal training, it is also connected with personal experience and insight—usually called expertise or wisdom.

Expert power can happen at many levels. People who have a lower position in an organizational or social hierarchy can have significant expert power based on knowing how to fill out request forms to get information or how to make travel arrangements; or from being up-to-date on issues affecting their position; or as a result of sharing information and getting the latest gossip about an initiative.

Examples of potential benefits accrued by engaging people with expert power	Examples of potential risks associated with the misuse of expert power
• The confidence that comes from knowing you have the best expertise possible to solve a problem or support an initiative • Avoiding red herrings in an initiative by having someone involved who has experience with most of them • Being able to contact a quick go-to person when urgent explanations or decisions are required	• Overdependence on one process perspective, resulting in an inherent bias • Unfair or excessive demands on expert volunteers who are donating their time and efforts • Overreliance on one way of looking at a problem (that is, from a recognized expert's point of view) rather than gathering input from those who may be affected by the problem in a different way and can provide another type of expertise or approach

Figure 4.6. Expert Power—Risks and Benefits

Resource Power

Resource power is the capacity to act and influence others based on access to a variety of resources such as human, financial, technological, educational, networks, or Web-based systems.

The powers in these resources may include budget-signing authority, having sufficient staff to carry out projects, having access to information technology experts and systems or to individuals or departments with expertise in the use of virtual technologies, and Web-based consulting and programming.

Examples of potential benefits accrued by engaging people with resource power	**Examples of potential risks associated with the misuse of resource power**
• Knowing what is needed to support a process and how to use resources intelligently • Access to what is needed when it is needed based on established priorities • Administrative support at levels sufficient to make an initiative run smoothly	• Assuming that new resources are required rather than thinking creatively about how to optimize existing resources • Using resources to manipulate what happens in a process (for example, when establishing priorities) rather than using established decision-making processes

Figure 4.7. Resource Power—Risks and Benefits

Relationship Power

Relationship power is the capacity to act and influence others based on relationships with people, or "who you know." Relationships may be with people who have sources of power different from yours, or they may be with family or friends. Relationship power can flow from shared experiences, integrity, mutual contacts, common interests, or family connections.

Examples include professional networks, a personal relationship with the chair of an advisory group in your organization, a family member who is well established in a field where you want to learn more.

Examples of potential benefits accrued by engaging people with relationship power	Examples of potential risks associated with the misuse of relationship power
• Tapping into networks and organizations to efficiently access individuals who can support projected outcomes • Personal knowledge about an individual's skills and abilities that enable a good fit with process requirements • Engaging a broad range of individuals in a community in various ways to support a process	• Having the same people involved on committees over long periods of time, thus becoming vulnerable to predictable suggestions and conclusions rather than exploring innovative approaches • Disparities associated with entrenched networks or relationships, leading to nepotism and other forms of inappropriate personal interest

Figure 4.8. Relationship Power—Risks and Benefits

Most stakeholders bring more than one of these eight types of power to a process. The president of a successful company who is a community leader and espouses strong values for corporate social responsibility and family support may have positional, personal, coercive, expert, resource, and relationship power. Given all these assets, individuals like this are usually in high demand as contributors to a broad range of committees and initiatives.

POWER AND COMMITMENT

Ideally, power and commitment go hand in hand. When powerful people are asked to make a commitment to an initiative, there is an implicit *give-get dynamic* in the relationship. That is, they will give their various types of power to support projected outcomes if they recognize that an initiative will get them support for their own values and goals. Making this relationship explicit and transparent supports the achievement of expectations for a process design.

A department head who sees unhealthy team dynamics as blocking achievement of financial goals would be likely to support a team development process (the give) designed to address financial challenges (the get) so that everyone involved can be successful. A philanthropist committed to environmental cleanup might agree to be a guest speaker and participant at a national conference (the give) with an objective to develop policies addressing contamination from oil spills (the get).

Having a discussion with stakeholders about give-get expectations in relation to the purpose and objectives of an initiative helps clarify the extent of their commitment to outcomes. It may also prevent disruptive interventions later on if the outcomes of a process don't line up as well with stakeholder expectations as initially thought.

Key Points for Commitment Discussions

- How the person came to be on the committee: volunteered, assigned by supervisor, invited or commandeered by a mentor, friend, colleague

- Experience with the purpose and objectives: several years in related areas, new to the area, personal involvement in a related issue

- Amount of time to commit: one day per month, a few hours per week, on an as-required basis to support a committee

- Length of commitment: for a few weeks, for a few months, for one year, over the length of the initiative

- Commitment to the outcomes of the initiative: only if they support personal goals and values; based on whatever the group decides by consensus; perhaps not committed to implementation, only to the preliminary process

USING POWER POSITIVELY

For many reasons, power may not be used positively to support a process: the people who have the power you need may not be available; you may not have the resources to get the people on your first-choice list; norms such as mutual respect and transparency about information may not be in place among planning committee members.

To support power being used positively:

- Ensure that roles and responsibilities of everyone involved are clear and recorded somewhere for easy and continual access. Develop a simple letter of agreement outlining these roles and responsibilities when people sign on to the initiative.

- Check out stakeholder commitment to the purpose, objectives, core assumptions, and key considerations in a process. Are the stakeholders clearly on board or are they hedging on their commitment? If the latter is true, clarify "without prejudice" where the lack of commitment is and explain clearly what is required to support the process as a whole.

- Name and describe the norms for working together, including specific examples of how those norms work in practice.

- If possible, avoid engaging powerful but high-maintenance people—people whose egos and personal needs are likely to get in the way of what you want to accomplish as a group or team. If this is not possible:

  - Look for ways in which these individuals can contribute positively without being obstructive.

  - Clarify key aspects of how people will be working together such as how decisions will be made and who has what authority.

  - Candidly discuss the challenges involved in working collaboratively given the situation for the initiative; ask the individuals involved whether they are comfortable working with these challenges throughout the time period of the initiative.

- Think about power strategically with respect to the purpose and objectives of the process: is it better to have a small committee with power concentrated in a few people who wear several hats and bring several types of power to the table? Or is it better to have a larger and more inclusive committee with power spread out among several individuals?

> The most efficient committees have the smallest number of individuals possible who can bring to the table the broadest perspectives and the specific types of power required to get the highest-quality work done in the time provided.

PROPOSITIONS

13. The positive use of power enables positive politics among stakeholders.

14. If outcomes are unimportant, then who brings what type of power to a process to enable achievement of outcomes is also unimportant.

15. Overdependence in process consulting can result in unnecessary and potentially harmful client-stakeholder-consultant relationships.

16. Powerful individuals without a commitment to established outcomes are high-maintenance wild cards.

4

5 The Values Factor in Process Design

Process design engages people in understanding how their values look in action. It offers people opportunities to address ongoing organizational and interorganizational issues, consult with stakeholders, and build agreement and ownership around important initiatives. Throughout all these processes, people—and the values they bring—are rarely in agreement.

Consider the following case. The dean of a department in a state college initiated a strategic planning process. A key decision involved who should participate in the final workshop: all faculty (fifty-three people) or only full-time faculty (twenty-one). Several part-time faculty members were high-profile, well-published academics who brought significant energy, credibility, and students to the school and assumed they would be participating in the workshop.

The external process consultant discussed the pros and cons of who should attend and how that might happen and made it clear that he thought it made sense to include both full- and part-time faculty. The dean also expressed a commitment to an inclusive approach. As it turned out, the dean (as the primary client) decided to restrict the retreat to full-time faculty. She based her decision on considerations such as the budget for the retreat, related processes that were engaging part-time faculty, multiple demands on people's time, and current labor issues regarding full- and part-time faculty status and related salaries. When the decision was communicated, several full- and part-time faculty made clear their disagreement with it.

The resulting challenge for the process consultant was to develop and facilitate a design to achieve expected outcomes in a difficult situation in which there were clear differences related to who should be included in the retreat. Although both the consultant and the client expressed their mutual ongoing commitment to a core value for inclusion, the final decision was a pragmatic one. If this dispute was not addressed in the process design, in all likelihood the success of the strategic planning process would be jeopardized.

> Exploring values in process design enables us to listen in a new way and with greater understanding to all aspects of a process.

As a result, the design needed to accommodate issues and related questions arising from this difference:

- Will this decision affect the integrity of the overall strategic planning process? How?

- How strongly do full- and part-time faculty feel about this issue?

- Should the dean's decision be taken to the planning committee for discussion?

- Are there other ways that part-time faculty can contribute to the planning process? (Through a pre-workshop questionnaire or interview, for example.)

- Can a way be found to involve both full- and part-time faculty in the workshop? (By inviting a representative sample of each group, for example.)

- Who will explain how the department's well-known value of inclusiveness was interpreted for this particular planning process?

- How could the design be developed to support workshop participants in discussing this decision and moving forward to work together in good faith?

- How should we communicate the results of this process in support of next steps?

> Peoples' values affect how they participate in processes. Change processes by their very nature make similarities and differences in values more obvious. These distinctions—which reflect value tensions—ensure that issues get agenda time.

5

ABOUT VALUES

Values are beliefs about what is desirable; they are deeply held within each individual. People's values guide how they participate in a process and how they direct their energies toward outcomes. Participants in processes manifest their values in many ways—for example, through their attitudes, intentions, judgments, behaviors, thinking, and the language they use.

Facts (what is) and values (what ought to be) are radically different. Values are concepts of the desirable, and facts are whatever is indisputably the case. Consequently, a value cannot be derived from a fact, as suggested in the statement "Let the facts speak for themselves," because facts never "speak for themselves." In other words, echoing Hume, you can't get an *ought* from an *is*.

Different observers often attribute different values to the same facts, if only for the simple reason that everyone experiences the world from a different perspective and the world comes up differently each time for each person. Therefore, in a fundamental sense, values are usually in conflict.

> The essential point to grasp is that values do not exist in the world. They are phenomenological, subjective, aspects of personal experience located within an individual. We are inclined to forget that any object such as a gold coin or the Mona Lisa is valueless and worthless save as we go through the exercise of attributing value to it. . . . The values which are attributed to such objects, facts, or events are at the will of the possessors, actors, beholders, participants.
>
> —Hodgkinson, 1983, p. 31.

A Values Continuum

Values can be seen as being on a continuum from posted to operative (Figure 5.1). People usually talk about or post their values—like notes on a bulletin board—as an initial step toward making them operational. When people act congruently with the values they espouse, their values are fully operational.

> To paraphrase Plato, a thing is not valued because it is good, it is good because it is valued.

5

1	2	3	4	5
Posted				Operative

Figure 5.1. Values Continuum—Posted to Operative

Think about a core value you have with respect to process consulting: for example, mutual respect, inclusiveness, transparency, integrity. Based on your work over the past year, how operative is this value?

Keep in mind that few values are fully operational all the time. It takes considerable experience and commitment to make conscious, values-based choices, particularly in the fast-paced and often ambiguous world of design and facilitation where competing demands are the norm. In addition, as people learn more about a field such as process consulting, they discover new ways to act on existing values and they take on (post) or espouse values that require new insights, skills, and practice to make fully operational. This can take both time and effort and is one reason why process consulting is so rewarding: it offers enough learning—particularly about how to operationalize values—to last a lifetime.

Integrity, Authenticity, and Mutual Respect

As process consultants, we hold three core values that guide how we work: integrity, authenticity, and mutual respect. *Integrity* reflects professional honesty, fairness, and objectivity. *Authenticity* is about being genuine—being sincere and caring with yourself and others. *Mutual respect* is about making the effort to understand people, honoring their rights and perspectives.

Our role is to model these values and enable their implementation when working collaboratively with others to develop, design, and implement healthy and productive processes. Implementing values requires the development of practical skills combined with patience and personal insight about behavior change. With experience, our understanding of these three values continually matures and deepens, yielding new insights and applications about the skills required to live these values on a day-to-day basis (Strachan, 2007, p. 32).

A VALUES HIERARCHY

A values hierarchy enables reflection and discussion about what the values are in relation to a process, who holds these values, and at what level they function. It also enables process consultants to listen for and understand people's value positions—what they see as desirable with respect to issues and outcomes. The hierarchy is not about judging value positions—it is instead an analytical tool for exploring, discussing, and checking your understanding of values conflicts and congruencies and their implications for process design.

From lowest to highest, the four levels of values are preference, consensus, consequence, and principle (Figure 5.2) (Hodgkinson, 1991, p. 97).

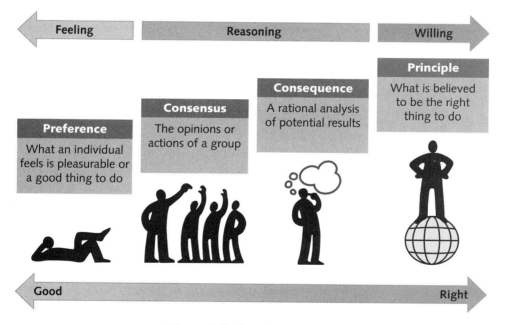

Figure 5.2. Levels of Values

Understanding and applying this hierarchy enables process consultants to respond to the question, Why is something *desirable,* that is, good or right? The answer involves an analysis of levels of values.

Level 1: Preference

Values held at the level of preference are based on what is pleasurable or a good thing to do for the individual concerned. At this level something is good simply because you like or want it and prefer it over something else, and you justify it based on what you personally feel is good. Taking food as an analogy, you may eat potatoes because they taste good and you like the texture. This is a fairly laid-back position—it's a preference. Similarly, some process consultants prefer to serve tap water instead of bottled water in workshops.

Level 2: Consensus

Values held at the level of consensus are based on the opinions and actions of a group. At this level the needs, interests, and demands of others come into play. This signifies a shift from what you personally feel is good to what the group wants—a matter of considering the opinions of others. To continue the food analogy, you may choose potatoes because a lot of people in your area (and in particular your friends) like them—they are a popular menu item in local restaurants—there is general agreement (consensus) that they're good to eat. Similarly, some process consultants ask for tap water on tables because they find that most participants are comfortable with it, and they see it as part of current conservation trends.

Level 3: Consequence

Values held at the level of consequence are based on a rational analysis of potential results. At this level, consideration of outcomes determines choices. Discussions frequently contain if-then propositions, and are often based on what the evidence says. In the food analogy, those who know that potatoes contain vitamins that contribute to good health will be inclined to choose them over something else. Similarly, process consultants who have read that nothing is wrong with tap water—and from a health perspective bottled water offers no particular advantage—will ask for

5

jugs of tap water on tables. At the same time, they need to be aware that any participants who are paraplegic will need special provisions, as people with this condition can usually manage bottles better than glasses of water.

Level 4: Principle

Values held at the level of principle are based on what people believe is the right thing to do. Something is right because it is proper, moral, duty bound, or simply what ought to be. Values held at this level are often codified into statements of belief, codes of ethics, or corporate values statements.

To complete the food analogy, people may eat potatoes because they were an important part of their family tradition and reflect the ancestral way of life on the farm. It's not a rational thing: it's about potatoes as a symbol of the importance of farming in an economy that often doesn't value the economics of agriculture. Similarly, process consultants who insist on tap water in workshops may do so because they believe in, are proud of, and support public water delivery systems in their community. They may provide sports bottles of tap water to accommodate participants who find glasses awkward to use.

Principle-based values are at the top of the hierarchy. This top level signifies a difference in approach between reasoning (consensus and consequence) and volition—that is, *willing* something to happen based on firmly established beliefs and attitudes that it is the right thing to do.

Holding to values at this level can involve refusing to go along with the will of the group (consensus) or to do what is considered rational (consequence). For example, most facilitators hold the value of mutual respect at this level and will

Clarity about philosophy and core values will help an organization maintain its integrity. Furthermore, since only those strategies consistent with an organization's philosophy and values are likely to work, the response to this question also helps the organization choose effective strategies.

—Bryson, 1988, p. 53

therefore not allow disrespectful behavior among participants in a design they are facilitating.

Looking at a process through the lens of a values hierarchy enables a different way of listening and acting. It is this form of listening and then applying the hierarchy to addressing issues that enriches the practice of process design and facilitation.

IMPLICATIONS FOR PROCESS DESIGN

Process design involves clients, stakeholders, and consultants in continual choices about a broad range of topics such as who to engage when about what; how decision making will happen; who should prepare a report; what assumptions should provide a basis for a process. Our values as process consultants guide how we make these choices in a very practical and visceral way. This requires us to clarify our values and their implications for our work and to listen for and confirm the values of clients, stakeholders, and participants in relation to issues—so that we can design and facilitate processes with these views in mind.

> We are unlikely to understand any behavior if it is seen only as a matter of individual moral choice detached from any social context. And we are unlikely to significantly increase honorable behavior if we rely only on individual rectitude. There is a kind of ecology of ethics. No matter how much you hector them, most Spartans will act like Spartans; most Athenians will act Athenian.
> —Cohen, 2002, p. 9

The guidelines that follow acknowledge the importance of knowing what values are at play in process design and how to make choices that address tensions and conflicts.

Here are five guidelines for process designers engaged in understanding and supporting clear values in an initiative:

- Listen for values.
- Clarify the extent to which values are operative.
- Identify and explore values-related tensions.
- Check the fit between you and your client.
- Choose a supportive decision-making process.

80

Listen for Values

Values manifest themselves in the challenges, issues, turning points, or tensions between and among participants and groups. Process designers are often aware of these tensions and who they involve but may not think about them in an organized way in relation to values. When listening for values, be sure to check out inferences to confirm their legitimacy.

Listen to language. Determining levels at which values are held is a subjective activity that involves honest, critical reflection. Stakeholders' language in these conversations can be revealing. For example:

- Principle: "My bottom line is. . . . "

- Consequence: "If you do this, then here's what will happen—and we can't afford to take that risk."

- Consensus: "We could keep on talking forever, but it sounds like everyone here could live with. . . . "

- Preference: "At a gut level I prefer option #1 for my group. It feels like it'll be a lot less hassle."

Attend to nonverbal indicators. Value intentions can be subtly expressed. When you listen carefully, you're apt to pick up on body language and other nonverbal clues that may lead you to hear that a comment made at the level of preference is more about consequence than preference, or that input provided at the level of principle is not as strong as it sounds. Be sure to check out any inferences you make about what you notice.

Keep the values hierarchy in mind. A value may be held at any level, and it is not always easy to determine at which level a person, group, or organization may hold a particular value. For example, mutual respect among individuals in a process can be based on:

- What is regarded as the right thing to do (principle): "Do unto others as you would have them do unto you."

- Reasoning (consequence): "If people are treated well they will work together more effectively than if they are disrespected. This is a good thing to do that results in the right action."

5

- Group norms (consensus): "Everyone knows that mutual respect is a good starting point for working together."

- Preference (feeling): "I feel better about myself and others when we all respect each other, although I can still get the work done if I have to do it with difficult people."

Identify whether a conflict is within one level of the value hierarchy (preference, consensus, consequence, or principle), between levels of the hierarchy, or both.

Ask about levels of values using the language of your client and key stakeholders. When discussing the values hierarchy, be sensitive to language. Just as you might not explain the research on stages of group development with a client when creating a design, you may not want to get into technical language about values. Ask the questions that follow while being sensitive to your client's language norms.

- What are the key conflicts that need to be accounted for in the process design?

- Is there a principle-level value involved?

- Does the existing conflict need to be addressed in this situation? Or can the participants live with the unresolved tensions?

- If certain people were not present, would the conflict be reduced significantly or eliminated altogether?

- Is there a need for additional information with respect to the conflicts involved? (Consider rules, professional standards, common practices, and political interests both inside and outside the participating organizations and groups.)

- In what ways does the conflict fall within clients' and stakeholders' zone of indifference?

The "zone of indifference" is the area within which people are willing to live with a situation. Perhaps they see the values in operation as "how things are done around here" and therefore OK for all practical purposes. Or they may not be motivated enough or committed enough to the issues to get engaged seriously and consider going against the grain to do what is right.

5

Clarify the Extent to Which Values Are Operative

It takes ongoing reflection and thoughtful action to make values drive decision making. Process designs can be helped or hindered by the extent to which stakeholder values are operative.

Identify and address differences between posted and operative values. Let's say that your client, who is the CEO of an organization, tells senior managers that a marketing-based planning process is the most important item on their agenda this year. However, the CEO then doesn't show up for the two main workshops for that initiative, even though they require top-level input and commitment. The role of the process designer in this situation is to have a conversation with the CEO about the importance of the leadership role in this initiative and to explore why those sessions were skipped. Does the CEO have an important reason for not being present? Or is the importance of marketing over the next twelve months a posted value but not an operative priority? And is the CEO aware that senior managers may interpret these actions as signaling willingness to talk about leadership and values but not to act on them?

Check out how operative key values are with your client and key stakeholders in the early stages of process design. When thinking about what values are required to support a design, ask your client how operative those values are. Tailor your language to suit the corporate culture: these discussions need not include the word *values* if it's not commonly used. For example, "To do a good job here and realize these outcomes, we need employees to be able to make a commitment to meeting these time lines. Do you have a tradition for that around here?"

Normalize discussions about values in relation to a process design. Identify and comment on the degree to which organizational values are operational and their potential for impact on a process design. If a corporation values teamwork, posts that value to employees, and works diligently at operationalizing it, then the designer should be able to perceive the potential support that value can have with respect to a process being developed in collaboration with employees.

On the other hand, if a value for teamwork is posted but only in the early stages of becoming operative, then the designer may want to look for ways that the process under development can contribute to making that value operative: a win-win for both client and consultant.

5

Identify and Explore Tensions

Tensions and conflicts are a normal and predictable part of organizational life. Look for and explore them when designing processes so that you can understand how they are based on participants' values, address them, and avoid surprises down the road.

Use facilitation tools to identify and discuss tensions. For example, a force-field analysis provides a way to identify the driving and restraining forces that bear on an issue: this process can be an invitation to discuss the value differences in play. Another way to identify conflicts is to ask your client and stakeholders what related aspects of the current situation have a lot of energy and could take everyone off topic.

More often than not, these tools are not described as being directly related to values clarification. You need to bring a values perspective and awareness about types of values to them to make them work for you in a design. For example, if you are using a give-get analysis in a team development session, you will be able to hear people's values resonating in their comments about what they value giving to and getting from a process.

When values conflict, explore the levels at which the tension is happening. When stakeholders (who hold a range of perspectives) look at issues, it is normal and healthy for their values to conflict. When this happens, the first step is to determine (or listen for) what the conflicting positions are and the levels at which they are held.

When values are held at different levels and conflict emerges in relation to what to do, higher values should prevail over lower values:

- Principles should prevail over consequences.

- Consequences should prevail over consensus.

- Consensus should prevail over preferences.

If you are facilitating the development of a strategic plan, company values held at the level of principle prevail over departmental values at the level of consequence. For example, if a corporate value at the level of principle is safety, the marketing department wants to increase sales by lowering safety considerations on a product, and doing this would increase the level of risk to consumers, then the corporate value trumps the departmental value.

Values conflicts within levels are resolved by force of will, strength, or power. Within level one, disagreements are resolved through strength of preference. For example, if two committee members are planning a lunch menu at a workshop and one prefers yogurt with more strength than the other prefers ice cream, then the dessert is likely to be yogurt.

Within the consensus and consequence levels, disagreements are resolved through group persuasion (consensus) or through strength of argument (consequence). Both these levels involve reasoning. For example, if group members are deciding what to do about a staff training challenge and the support for one approach (in terms of data, experience, and persuasion) outweighs that for another, then the group decision will probably go with that approach.

Within the principle level, disagreements are resolved through force of will. For example, if legislators believe that seat belts can prevent suffering, save lives, and reduce health care costs without significant loss of personal freedom, then they will use their force of will to pass legislation to enforce seat belt use, regardless of the fact that public opinion (consensus) is not yet supportive or that conclusive research (consequence) is not quite in place.

Clarify how values may have shifted among the four levels. Values in process design and facilitation wax and wane among the four levels of the hierarchy in response to factors such as critical incidents, research, marketing, and the enthusiasm of professionals in organizational change and management development. For example, corporate social responsibility may be a value at the level of principle for several years because a book on that subject is on best-seller lists, only to be replaced by the value of employment diversity for similar reasons.

The senior leadership in organizations, alliances, and networks has a lot to do with which values are held at which level. If a new president is brought in to save an organization that is deemed to be inefficient, then efficiency is likely to be posted as a value at the level of principle very quickly. Similarly, if a company has just been convicted of illegal financial transactions resulting from overemphasis on financial efficiencies and the appearance of the balance sheet, it is fairly predictable that ethical financial practices will be posted at the level of principle in short order.

The more you know about the history and context of values in an organization, and what values are held at what level, the better you can design and facilitate processes to support desired outcomes that are aligned with organizational values. Having this information at your fingertips can also prevent unnecessary

5

discussion or interventions later on: you know up front that the process design must reflect the core values of the organization.

Make conscious decisions about which tensions should be addressed. In a process focused on practical social solutions in low-resource communities, exclude issues that may be held at the level of principle and are not amenable to management or resolution—why people are poor, for example—and focus on those that can be resolved, such as the development of alternative low-cost housing options for people on medical disability insurance.

Similarly, when a group's leadership has identified aspects of an issue that are unresolvable in the current context, consider taking that aspect of the issue off the agenda. For example, in a planning session you might say, "Given the current situation, human resources should be considered as status quo for the next twelve months."

Proceed with caution when a conflict is at the level of preference. Preference values are personal; we all justify them on the basis of how we feel about an issue. As such, they are self-gratifying. Rational, significant choices—particularly the type involved in complex processes that require significant time and energy—are not often perceived to be a priority for those who are involved in conflicts they hold at a level of preference.

When a majority of participants in a process hold their values about an issue at the level of preference, they may not have a significant stake in building agreement. The process design challenge is to determine whether participants can be engaged in what is at stake and therefore develop the energy required to address the issue, or whether coming to agreement on the issue is simply not as important to them as it is to the client.

It's tricky to design engagement strategies for people who aren't committed to building agreement. Although the possibility of their developing a renewed sense of commitment is always present, so is the danger that you are getting people engaged primarily for the purpose of the process itself rather than for a legitimate longer-term goal. If this is the case, then perhaps the client and consultant involved should spend time exploring whether the process has integrity for participants over the longer term.

Think carefully about taking on values conflicts at the level of principle. An important facet of the art of process consulting is knowing when to raise and when to avoid questions of principle.

Conflicts entrenched at the level of principle are difficult, if not impossible, to resolve: this type of value conflict is the defining feature of a moral dilemma. Ultimately these are (or eventually become) power struggles among key value actors. These ultimate conflicts often end up being resolved or managed temporarily through force of will, positional power, or physical aggression to protect even higher values such as social justice or personal safety.

> We often recognize an intractable values conflict intuitively first. Something just doesn't feel right about the process as a whole. It's only after getting more information that we can explain rationally why that is the case.

One memorable contract involved facilitating the merger of two nongovernment organizations with significant mandate overlap. Our sense was that all parties involved came into the process with significant goodwill and the desire to take a collaborative, consensus-based approach to the process. Within six months, however, it became clear that the two CEOs involved held different positions at the level of principle, were firmly entrenched in support of those positions, and refused to accommodate the merger process. Eventually both were terminated, and an outside CEO was hired to lead the new organization. The dilemma was resolved based on the positional power of the board chair whose position (held at the level of principle) was a newly merged, combined, and efficient organization with a happy workforce.

To be successful in addressing issues at the level of principle, find aspects of the issue that can be resolved at lower levels where a rational discussion can hold sway. For example, harking back to the faculty off-site discussed at the beginning of the chapter, "Although our mission statement is committed to equity in participation, perhaps we don't all have to participate in the same way by attending the main forum. Would you consider involving some people through a consultation and others through a questionnaire and still others through phone interviews so that we have a smaller and more efficient number at the final session?"

If you don't see a way to facilitate the lowering of a values conflict from the level of principle to a rational discussion based on consensus or consequence, then there may be little likelihood for you to contribute to a successful resolution in that situation. This may be the time to discuss whether process design and facilitation is appropriate for that particular situation.

5

Have a frank discussion with your client: describe your conclusions about the organization's core values. For example, "I'm observing that we are talking about this particular issue in terms of entrenched principles. However, to resolve this collaboratively we need to get to discussions related to outcomes and consequences and how to build agreement. There doesn't seem to be much movement in relation to this, and I'm concerned that this will keep us from achieving our objectives. What is your sense of the situation?"

Approach consensus- and consequence-level values conflicts with confidence. Values based on reasoning—consensus and consequence—are most amenable to process design and facilitation. These two levels are where people can review background information and explore each other's positions, and where collaborative processes can result in respectful and mutually supportive decision making.

> To quote a medical credo: First do no harm.

Consensus- and consequence-level values, although rationally determined, do not discount the importance of intuition in decision making. Intuition functions at all four levels. These two levels simply provide a strong entry point for design and facilitation, whereas level 1 (preference) and level 4 (principle) are imbued with obstacles to collaborative decision making.

Typical statements from stakeholders regarding how to design sessions involving values conflicts at these levels include: "We need to get the research and other background information required to make a good decision here" (consequence) or "Let's get all the perspectives on the table so that we can discuss this and agree on what to do" (consensus).

The challenge is to determine the degree to which each of these two levels should play a role in a process. Here are sample questions to determine your options in a policy development case example:

- Do stakeholders (for example, scientists and technicians) value evidence and professional expertise over group consensus? If yes, to what extent?

- Do stakeholders (for example, issue advocates and community developers) value group discussion and collaborative decision-making processes with a broad range of input over scientific evidence and expertise? If yes, to what extent? Do stakeholders value both of these levels equally?

5

- Do stakeholders value a specific balance between these two levels? For example, they may want to depend primarily on scientific research, but in situations where there isn't enough research to support a conclusion they will go with expert opinion.

Check the Fit Between You and Your Client

Clarify your approach to process design with your client. Do you customize each process, or do you advocate for a specific model to be used in most situations? If you specialize in one type of design or hold a way of designing and facilitating at the level of principle, this means that you apply that model or approach to all situations, and it is important to make your client aware of that fact.

From our perspective, no single model or approach works best in a majority of situations. We prefer to look at each situation as an individual challenge in the light of our options and skills. Decisions about which models, approaches, and technologies go into a design are based on a discussion with the client and stakeholders about what could be the best way to achieve outputs and outcomes given resources available and the values in operation.

Clients need to know your position on specific models and approaches as they reflect your values about process design and facilitation. Some clients have already decided what type of process they want in a situation. Other clients don't know what they want, or they may have an inkling about what will work for them but want to discuss it further. If you are clear about your values in relation to how you do process design, you are better prepared to decline work opportunities that don't fit with them—or to accept such opportunities when countervailing factors apply.

Even when you have the experience, expertise, and confidence to do what a client wants done, it can be confusing to consider whether you should take on a piece of work that is surrounded by potentially difficult circumstances and may not line up perfectly with your values.

A few years ago a faith-based national organization asked us to research, design, and facilitate a national board development process focused on current issues that had become increasingly conflicted over the preceding six months. We discussed the work in our company and, when we met with the president of the organization, mentioned that we weren't sure that we were the right group to do this work because we had very different views from theirs on a specific social issue.

5

The president of the organization responded that he wanted us to work with him and the board as process consultants (research, design, facilitation) based on what he had seen us do in a similar situation. He said that since that social issue was not one of the challenges they wanted us to address, he assumed that we would bring our professional objectivity to the work and that he was confident that things would go well. And then he suggested that we needed to take a few days to reflect on our values as process consultants and whether we would be comfortable making a commitment to do this work.

After considerable discussion and reflection we took on this contract. This work resulted in a very rich and rewarding relationship with that organization and subsequently with others of different faiths. The fit turned out well for all involved.

Nonetheless, whether you are an internal or external consultant, much is at stake when you take on work that doesn't fit your values, experience, expertise, or schedule.

Here are some options for reflecting on the fit between you and a potential client in both internal and external process consulting opportunities:

- I have done this before several times and this sounds like it would be a good fit: our values and skills seem congruent.

- I appreciate your confidence in my skills in this area. Who else do you know in our department whose skills would complement mine and who might want to work with me on this?

- I've done similar work before with this group, and I think it's time for fresh eyes. This is a longstanding values issue that seems to be attached to a couple of key senior managers who are not moving on. Several employees have said outright that nothing would persuade them to change their positions on this issue. I suggest you work with a colleague of ours on this process.

- I am not convinced that this type of problem will benefit from a facilitated process. You may want to consider an intervention by your human resources department or perhaps mediation or negotiation rather than facilitation.

- Bring it on! This is right up my alley, and I can't wait to get started.

5

Choose a Supportive Decision-Making Process

Knowing stakeholder values in relation to decision making can support an appropriate decision-making process that enables knowledge transfer during and after the main workshop.

Explore stakeholders' values in relation to decision making. Different stakeholders value different types of decision-making processes. Some people may have a strong belief in the wisdom of group consensus due to its tendency to build ownership for outcomes. Others may value an opportunity for input followed by an authoritarian decision-making style for perceived implementation efficiency in the field. Still others may value an evidence-based, scientific approach to support professional ownership for conclusions.

The more you know about people's values related to decision making, the more input you have to help you set your design and facilitate how people can come to agreement on issues. For example, effective consensus decision making requires comprehensive information about potential consequences to ensure that participants have all the information they need to avoid groupthink and feel comfortable about their group decision after the process is complete (Janis, 1982).

Tailor decision making to each situation. Customize the decision-making process to reflect participants' realities. Professionals such as engineers, lawyers, and dentists—who have access to comprehensive information about clients in their day-to-day work—are accustomed to making decisions based on a lot of data and in a situation where they have significant control. It makes good sense to develop a decision-making strategy that accommodates these needs.

Think about facilitating a group of dental professionals. In their day-to-day work lives they review a comprehensive chart, X-rays, a dental history, and personal preferences for pain treatment, and then walk into a room where they are in complete control. Someone is sitting in a chair who will do everything they ask and is unable to comment about what they are doing or the decisions they are making until they are finished. The dentist says "Open" and the patient obeys—not even pausing to ask, "How wide?" It makes sense that a group like this, accustomed to so much information for decision-making purposes, would also like to have copious amounts of background information before making decisions in a planning process. When it comes to decision making, they hold comprehensive background information at the level of principle.

5

Be specific about the nature of evidence for decision making. To prevent misunderstandings in situations where the evidence for decision making is poor, facilitators can include an assumption in the process terms of reference such as, "Although we don't have the best science to support us in making a decision, given the urgency of this issue and our commitment to do more good than harm, we will proceed with this process and make decisions on the best evidence available, that is, expert opinion from world leaders in this field." This assumption accommodates these groups' appreciation of the need for best evidence in decision making, which they hold at the level of principle (see Chapter Sixteen).

IN SUMMARY

People's values—their beliefs about what is desirable—guide how they participate in a process design and how they direct their energies toward outcomes. The more awareness you have as a process consultant about the nature of choices in process design and how values guide those choices, the more consistent and grounded your decisions will be in collaboration with others and the more targeted the design will be to support anticipated outcomes.

In the final analysis, if you decide that a situation is not amenable to process design and facilitation, explain your assessment of the situation to the client or sponsor and key stakeholders, and explore some options with them:

- You decline to do the work.

- You and they reconstrue the project with a different, manageable scope.

- You and they decide to do nothing further on the project: take a wait-and-see approach.

- You and they wait for a specified period of time to see the impact of related initiatives and then reconvene to discuss the future of the project.

- They resolve the situation by asking someone (with the positional power required) to make a final decision about the contentious issue.

- You offer to bring your process design and facilitation skills to work in collaboration with people who have skills in other approaches such as mediation, conflict resolution, negotiation, reconciliation, or arbitration.

5

PROPOSITIONS

17. Value conflicts are the rule rather than the exception.

18. Reconciling the individual with the group or with the organization is central to addressing value conflicts.

19. Facts, perspectives, and values are essential to process design. Facts are discovered; perspectives are explored; values are exposed, clarified, and willed (Hodgkinson, 1996).

20. An important facet of the art of process consulting is knowing when to raise and when to avoid questions of principle.

21. Using process consulting skills to address disputes or issues in situations where conflicting values are held at the level of principle has the potential to do more harm than good.

5

3

DUE DILIGENCE: A PROCESS TERMS OF REFERENCE

Given the significant investment required by all involved to initiate, set up, and participate in a process, it is essential to have a comprehensive understanding of the main elements affecting its design and facilitation: the situation, focus, stakeholders, core assumptions, key considerations, work plan, governance, and essential documents. When due diligence has been done for each of these eight elements, the resulting process terms of reference (PTR) anchors the initiative, supporting a high standard of care in relation to discussion and decision making.

Part Three describes how to create a PTR. Each chapter is dedicated to one element and includes a detailed description of that element followed by sample questions for working with clients, practice guidelines, and case examples. The final chapter provides three examples of PTRs for different sectors.

6 About a Process Terms of Reference

A PTR is a framework for understanding eight key elements that affect how a design rolls out in the hands of a facilitator. These eight elements describe the situation, focus, stakeholders, core assumptions, key considerations, work plan, governance, and documentation for an initiative (Figure 6.1).

Completing a PTR in collaboration with stakeholders is the up-front work that is required to anchor a process. This work is essential to productive process design: it clarifies and shapes the conceptual heart of an initiative and the relationships, roles, and responsibilities required to make it successful.

Robust processes engage people from various perspectives in purposeful and rewarding ways. A quality PTR supports the art of process consulting: you're not relying on quick tips, established models, or handouts to frame your decision making—they are essential tools of the trade but not the essence of your work. The process PTR enables you to understand at a deep level exactly what is going on with whom and why, when, and where. Once that fundamental understanding is in place, the rest is pure tango.

MAPS AND TERRITORIES

Creating a PTR is like creating a map: the PTR tells you about the things that are most prominent and important to the initiative at hand; however, it doesn't tell you everything you will need to know.

Figure 6.1. A PTR at a Glance

The PTR is to the design as the map is to the territory; you need to walk through it and experience it with participants to really understand what it is about and how a design gets a life of its own when people start to explore the territory.

Frank Lloyd Wright knew how to design a building that fit beautifully into the key features of its surrounding landscape. Similarly, excellence in process design is about creating an agenda and detailed design that fit into the intended territory. The PTR makes that territory explicit: the more you know about the territory in which a process will play out, the more confident you will be in designing something that will accommodate all the surrounding hills and valleys—and those pesky pointed rocks just beneath the surface that aren't apparent initially.

In process design, as in travel, sometimes the map doesn't fit the territory and you encounter something unexpected. For example, a

> A map or guidebook does not 'solve' problems and does not 'explain' mysteries; it merely helps to identify them.
> —Schumacher, 1977, p. 8

bridge is out because of a storm a few hours ago, or a new road has been put in and the map hasn't been updated, or what initially looked like a minor dispute blossoms into a major values conflict. Recognizing the inevitability of a few surprises in a facilitated meeting and enjoying the energy and excitement involved in their appearance is based on understanding the relationship between the map and the territory.

In summary, a PTR serves several important functions:

- It gives you the information you need to decide whether the *fit* between you and your potential client is good. Whether you are working internally or externally, this information enables you to make a wise decision in this regard.

- It provides *a comprehensive map* for initiating a process. This helps to clarify and build mutual understanding before moving into action.

- It provides an ongoing *point of reference* as a process evolves and takes shape.

- It enables you to go *beyond the presenting issue* (what you learn initially about a problem) into a more comprehensive understanding of a situation.

- It enables you to find out to what extent the client or sponsor is a part of both the *problem and the solution,* whether in supporting or limiting ways.

- It supports stakeholders in raising and discussing the *taken-for-granted assumptions* ("how we do things around here") that are present in all processes. Uncovering and exploring these assumptions supports transparency and critical reflection as important norms for working together.

- It supports stakeholders in building *ownership and commitment* for the initiative.

6

- It prepares participants to be able to name the *values tensions* (discussed in Chapter Five) embedded in the issues being considered and where and how they are in conflict.

- It results in an insightful record for doing a *retrospective* or for exploring lessons learned with respect to future related processes.

As things change over time, refine the PTR to reflect what will happen in the session. If the PTR is for an initiative longer than the single session you are designing, review the objectives, outputs, and outcomes to make sure they also apply to that specific session.

DEVELOPING A PTR

Although the eight sections in a PTR are listed sequentially to organize thinking—starting with the situation and moving clockwise—developing this document can happen in many different ways.

Sometimes an initial meeting with a client begins with a discussion about stakeholders; at other times we start with a detailed orientation and proposed outcomes prepared by the client; in still other situations, we simply listen to the client describe the situation, take notes on several areas at once, and then later start to put a draft together that we will share with them and other stakeholders at the next meeting.

Some elements obviously need to come before others: it is easier to talk about what background information you need if you have clarity about the purpose and objectives. That being said, if a client wants to talk about a priority discussion document that has been developed to address the main issue in a process, then we would review that document and listen to how the client wanted to frame the process around the document.

In summary: there is no foolproof sequence for developing a PTR. Go to where your clients are: if they want to talk about the big picture first, great! That's where you start listening. If they prefer to describe important decisions leading up to a process, great! That's where you start listening. If they prefer to begin with outcomes, great! As the process consultant, you can organize the information into a PTR to understand it and reflect it back to others around the table.

6

A COLLABORATIVE STANCE

Regardless of where or how it starts, developing a PTR eventually involves setting up a table for collaboration where stakeholders from a range of perspectives and experiences can clarify and confirm each part of the PTR (Figure 6.2). In addition to supporting an inclusive dynamic for participants, a collaborative stance builds ownership for the process and helps to clarify expectations about what success will look like and require.

Although a collaborative approach to developing a PTR takes more time and energy up front, it can save a lot of time later on. As the old saying makes clear, "Bring me in early, I'm your partner. Bring me in late, I'm your judge."

How does a PTR differ from a project charter?

For the purposes of this book, a PTR clarifies and shapes the conceptual heart of an initiative, and the relationships, roles, and responsibilities required to make it successful. It is an essential leadership tool for designing and facilitating a process. The focus is on planning and decision making to support outcomes that fit established missions, visions, and values through a collaborative, stakeholder-driven process.

A project charter focuses on the steps required to manage and implement an initiative. The project charter and the PTR need to work hand in hand (and frequently

Figure 6.2. A Table for Collaboration
Tomlinson and Strachan, 2005.

6

overlap) to ensure that the purpose, objectives, boundaries, and intentions of an initiative don't drift off target.

When do you create a process PTR?

Much depends on the unique aspects of each situation. Ideally a PTR is developed during the start-up phase of an initiative. However, if you start to work on a process after it is under way and a PTR is not in place, developing one can provide an excellent catch-up intervention to ensure that everyone has the same baseline understanding.

We usually begin by taking notes on a PTR during initial discussions with the client and before the idea of a process PTR is on the table. The eight categories of the framework provide a useful listening tool for organizing thoughts during these initial conversations which often contain key insights, assumptions, and considerations, as well as important language specific to an initiative. After these discussions we prepare a working draft that is reviewed with a planning committee.

Other approaches work just as well. Some clients will provide you with a package of information prior to your first meeting with them, and you can begin to organize the PTR based on this data. Other clients and stakeholders like to begin with a completed sample PTR (like one of those in Chapter Fifteen) from another project so that they have a general idea of what is required.

Sometimes sections of a PTR will have been completed for another initiative. For example, key considerations may be described in a SWOT analysis (strengths, weaknesses, opportunities, threats) done for a related project, and that becomes a starting point. If the client has created a background information package, then our role is to make sure this information is clearly organized into the framework's eight elements so that we can move forward with the client on the design.

Regardless of when you start to create this document, the goal is early and continual participation with the client and a few key stakeholders to build ownership for the PTR as a touchstone throughout an initiative.

Who should be involved in creating and seeing a PTR?

By taking a consciously collaborative approach to developing a PTR, process designers and facilitators can increase participation and ownership, build synergies, and enable the development of strategies to accommodate strengths and weaknesses among stakeholders. All this helps build an inclusive approach to discussion and decision making throughout an initiative.

6

Work with the smallest group of individuals that can provide a useful range of perspectives on the initiative (as discussed in Chapter Nine), usually a number between three and ten. The larger the group, the more difficult it is to organize meetings.

What works for us is to have a very small group of three or four key players (with different perspectives) create the PTR and then have it reviewed by a larger advisory group, again representing a range of perspectives. Regardless of the group's size, it is essential that the client, stakeholders, and process consultant each respect what the others bring to the table.

The PTR is not developed for broad distribution. It is intended for use by those involved in planning and steering the process. Specific parts are distributed to specific groups: the purpose, objectives, outputs, and outcomes usually go to workshop participants, as do the assumptions and sometimes the key considerations. Avoid distributing too much information too widely.

How much time does it take to develop a PTR?

Spending time at the front end to create a PTR is upstream prevention: it helps make sure that less time is required later on for interventions that could have been avoided. The time required to develop, revise, and finalize a PTR varies from a few hours to several days and longer, depending on size and complexity and whether you are an internal or external process consultant.

A number of factors are involved:

- How well you know the client and the situation: if you are an internal manager or consultant, you are probably familiar with most of the information required to complete a PTR; if you are external, you are likely to have a lot to learn.

- Whether you have worked with this client, group, committee, team, or organization before.

- How complex the process is.

- How many people are involved.

- The nature of relationships and norms for working together.

- Who needs to be consulted.

- How long the challenge has existed.

- Whether there is a commitment to address the challenge.

6

> It took us about ten weeks, several drafts, and three teleconferences to develop a terms of reference for a sensitive national consensus-building process. Every minute we spent on it paid off in the end. Although it was frustrating at times, going through this exercise made sure we were all on the same wavelength. We clarified the key issues up front with both the steering and planning committees so that they didn't pop up unexpectedly later.
>
> —A Stakeholder

How you develop a PTR can be a big help when it comes to implementing outcomes: stakeholders are writing the songbook that they're going to sing from throughout the entire initiative and during implementation.

How long is an average PTR?

The length of a PTR depends on the scope and complexity of an initiative. Some are between two and four pages (for a single facilitation) while others are much longer (twenty and more pages for a complex, phased, multi-session, year-long intervention).

Create a PTR regardless of the length and size of the initiative. Sometimes short processes for a limited number of participants can have a greater strategic impact than larger processes involving many more people: they all need to be thought through clearly.

PRACTICE GUIDELINES: DEVELOPING A PTR

How you develop a PTR is as important as what gets included. The way people relate to one another when developing the PTR sets a precedent for how they will continue to work together throughout an initiative.

Clarify and maintain your role as a process consultant, that is, designer and facilitator. While preparing a PTR, the role of the process consultant is to attend to group process and enable collaboration while keeping the document up to date as a go-to reference tool for the client and stakeholders. Whether you are internal or external, this involves

- Confirming and supporting the project mandate

- Keeping the initiative on track and on time

- Guiding deliberations and decision making in committee work

- Supporting focused and healthy interpersonal communication among stakeholders

- Enabling transparency regarding core assumptions (defined in Chapter Ten) and key considerations (Chapter Eleven), thereby deepening and raising the level of work

- Contributing to an in-depth understanding of fundamental issues affecting the initiative

During the development of a PTR, the objective or neutral process consultant (whether internal or external) is impartial, fair, and unbiased with respect to the content being discussed. Consultants may have their own opinions on the content, but they should not let that personal bias unduly influence group decision making. This participant-observer stance makes it possible to observe what is happening, notice group dynamics, track the development of content, and acknowledge personal opinions while staying firmly grounded in the contract with the client and the group (Strachan, 2007, pp. 34–35).

> With clients who are new to the role of a process consultant it can be helpful to clarify the difference between a *chairperson* and a *process consultant,* and to spell out the role that objectivity plays in process design and facilitation.

It may occasionally be appropriate for a process consultant to take on the role of expert. For example, if you have information on a subject that would be useful to participants, you may want to step out of your role as a process consultant and provide that information. In these situations, be clear about your change in role so that everyone involved understands that you are temporarily setting aside your objectivity. And keep in mind that if this change in role happens too frequently, participants can become confused about who is doing what, and how that will influence decision making.

6

Prepare carefully for the first meeting to develop a PTR.

The first meeting provides an opportunity for stakeholders to discuss what they bring to the table, what they want to get out of an initiative, and how they see their involvement throughout the process. They need to see themselves and their expectations reflected in the PTR.

Depending on how the first meeting is set up, you can customize the following questions to help build this table for collaboration:

- What are our expectations for involvement in this process—for example, time commitment, decision making, leadership?
- How can we develop a common language—for example, shared meaning of terms, acronyms, concepts, attitudes?
- What are the potential opportunities and benefits, costs, and limitations for each of us as a result of working collaboratively at this table?
- What are our ground rules for working together—for example, communication, confidentiality, mutual respect, transparency, boundaries of individuals and the interests they represent?
- How can we ensure that stakeholder roles and responsibilities with respect to the initiative are clear, understood, relevant, and specific to our initiative?
- How will we identify and address potential conflicts—for example, conflicts of interest, or differences with respect to priorities and personalities?
- How will we know that our collaboration has been successful?

Maintain a developmental, iterative perspective.

In theory, a PTR involves a logical step-by-step approach. What happens in practice is a synchrony of information coming from several perspectives at the same time. It is common to be working on one section (such as context) when important aspects of another section (such as stakeholders) are raised.

Be prepared to go through several iterations of a PTR, revisiting and refining it as the situation evolves. Date each PTR and keep previous versions. Participants often revisit earlier discussions and decisions, and it is useful to have a record of how the PTR has matured during the life of a process.

If a PTR or some part of it—often the purpose and objectives—is presented to you already completed by your clients, ask how it was developed. Then go through it in detail with them, asking whose perspectives are included or excluded

6

and explaining the benefits of taking an inclusive, developmental approach. Ensure that a draft PTR is reviewed by others with a stake in the process.

Check for congruence among all eight elements in a PTR. For example, check the objectives in the PTR against other sections such as noticing which background documents serve the achievement of which objectives or which key considerations will affect discussions and outcomes of which objectives. Recheck revisions to the PTR against the purpose and objectives to ensure the process remains aligned.

Do a final review of the PTR with your planning committee prior to finalizing the design. In particular, ask if there have been any new developments regarding assumptions and key considerations that might have an impact on the success of the process.

Pay attention to levels of abstraction.

A PTR is designed to be clear, focused, and specific. Notice the level of abstraction in discussions and call attention to it when it is inappropriate.

For example, if the purpose of a process is to identify specific strategies to help people on medical disability insurance find affordable housing, then abstract discussions lamenting the causes of poverty are not likely to be very helpful. Similarly, if the purpose of a process is to develop high-level strategic sales goals and participant discussions are focused at an operational level, call attention to this fact to get people back on track.

Interventions that remind people about the purpose and scope of an initiative help support an appropriate level of abstraction in discussions.

Build ownership for outcomes.

Ownership develops when people are involved, when they have a hand in shaping a PTR and are participating in decisions about how things will happen—this is when they start to take responsibility for outcomes. To support the development of ownership it is helpful to know whether committee members have taken on their roles voluntarily or have been assigned to do the work, as this may influence how they want to be engaged.

Maintain boundaries between the PTR and the process itself such as specific workshops.

When facilitating the development of a PTR for a workshop, stay focused on the PTR and avoid discussions about design or facilitation that belong in the workshop. To keep your committee focused on the PTR you may need to ask, "Are we talking about the PTR here? Or have we moved into the actual workshop?"

6

PROPOSITIONS

22. A PTR surfaces what matters, including what is said and not said, what is seen and not seen, what is done and not done.

23. The map is not the territory. The PTR is not the design. The design is not the process.

24. The process reflects how the PTR manifests itself in the design.

25. Multiple levels of interests and concerns that emerge in the development of a PTR reflect potential implementation challenges.

26. When creating a PTR, discussions about competing and ambiguous purposes, objectives, and outcomes help build rigor.

27. Decisions made in a PTR may result in consequences that can't be predicted or controlled.

28. Designing and facilitating contentious issues without a PTR is like crossing a busy street with your eyes closed.

29. To paraphrase Churchill, we shape our process designs and then they shape us.

6

7 Understanding the Situation

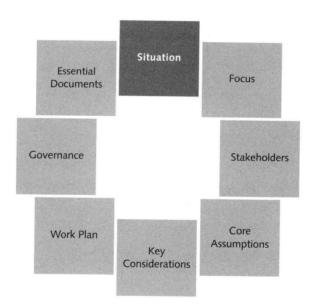

The situation section of a PTR introduces you to the circumstances and context in which a process exists. It helps to reveal the meaning of a process in relationship to its setting, key stakeholders, and contributing factors.

The situation section includes

- Circumstances and conditions surrounding the process
- A rationale for doing the process at this time

- A brief history outlining key events leading up to the initiative
- A list of the clients
- A general statement about the main challenge—for example, planning, team development, visioning
- Potential benefits to key stakeholders and larger constituencies

SAMPLE QUESTIONS FOR EXPLORING THE SITUATION

How ready is this organization or community of stakeholders to take on this process? How do you know this?

What has happened in the past few years that has led to where you are now?

What is the justification for the time and expense involved in this process?

What needs will this initiative address for our customers?

What needs will this initiative address for the communities we serve?

What's going on now that prompted you to initiate this process? or What stories can you tell that demonstrate the need for this process?

Who initiated this process and what motivated them to do that?

Who stands to benefit from this process and how might that happen?

Who stands to lose from this process and how might that happen?

Who will use the results and for what purpose? Who else might be interested in the results of this process?

PRACTICE GUIDELINES: SITUATION

- Check all the *facts and the wording* in this section, quoting from official documents whenever possible. Build agreement among stakeholders so that *excerpts can be used later* for letters of invitation, briefing notes, announcements.
- Developing this section *with stakeholders* can prevent misperceptions later on, for example, ensuring that partners and sponsors are described clearly and accurately, and profiled equitably.

- Clarify up front *who your clients are,* particularly who has the authority to make which decisions. It helps to think about specific types of clients (discussed in Chapter Three) when considering responsibility and accountability for a process.

- Create a point form, easy-to-read *chronology* leading up to the process so that everyone has the same understanding of past events. Verify the chronology with key stakeholders prior to distributing it.

  - Make a link to past processes, what decisions were made and how those decisions led to this initiative.

  - Describe what is currently going on that helps to reveal the meaning of this process.

  - Describe what will be happening after this process and how those events are linked to this initiative.

  - Include what people need to know that will give meaning to this initiative from their perspectives; for example, why this process is happening now.

- Think and act *inclusively:* each type of client has a perspective on any initiative. In some settings, particularly in smaller shops, the same person is more than one type of client. For example, the contacting client may also be the primary client.

- Keep the situation section fairly *general;* avoid getting into specific issues, opportunities, considerations, and assumptions, all of which are addressed later in the PTR.

- Take stock regularly while preparing this section: is this *a good fit* for your skills and experience?

> In reality, the question of who is actually the client can be ambiguous and problematical. One can find oneself not knowing whom one is working for, or working with several clients whose goals are in conflict with each other. And, as the consultation or managerial process evolves over time, the question of who is *really* the client becomes more and more complicated.
>
> —Schein, 1987, p. 117.

7

EXAMPLES: SITUATION

Strategic Planning: Urban Law Firm with Eighteen Partners

As managing partner of this firm (primary client), I have been clear with the partners that this year's strategic planning process is both urgent and timely. Given the decision to close our family practice section, in addition to internal conflicts and increased pressure in the marketplace, we need to come to agreement on a new vision, review and decide on key areas of practice, and confirm how we want to work together over the next five years.

Our client satisfaction ratings continue to be high. We know that we are providing good service at a fair price. However, revenues have been declining at about 4 percent per year for the last three years while expenses are rising 3 percent annually. The presence of two new firms in town that focus on areas similar to ours is another challenge: is this an opportunity or a heightened risk?

The largest bookstore in our community is enjoying record profits in its paraprofessional section. People are buying how-to books on law, medicine, accounting, divorce, and contracting, and these books are now including do-it-yourself templates on CDs. When you couple this development with the plethora of legal information on the Web, it is clear that we need to rethink our corporate vision and how we want to be perceived in our community. Can we create products of value to our clients that don't involve us billing them for time?

Although this process involves our partners (our ultimate client) in taking a strategic look at pressing long-term issues and answers, we also need to be clear about how our decisions will be implemented from a management perspective. This may involve rethinking current staff assignments as part of this planning process.

7

Issues-Based Planning: State Psychiatric Hospital

Reform of the prison system in our state is a high priority for the governor (primary client) and the Democratic Party. Well-supervised, earlier parole for psychiatric offenders was a key part of last year's election platform, and we have a commitment to deliver the systemic and organizational change required to make that platform a reality within five years.

The partners involved in the operation of the State Psychiatric Hospital have different perspectives on how the institution should be managed. There is an underlying conflict between the health treatment orientation of psychiatrists, nurses, and orderlies, who bring a hospital perspective to the table, and the confinement perspective of security personnel and their respective unions.

Although data on recidivism for psychiatric offenders clearly supports the governor's position both in terms of public safety and cost-benefit analysis, the popular media do not provide positive coverage on successful reintegration of psychiatric offenders into the community. This coverage simply does not sell newspapers.

In the past three months, the media in our state have provided high-profile coverage on the case of a sex offender released last year from our hospital who recently re-offended and has been convicted of rape. Public opinion polls are pressuring all state psychiatric hospitals to review and tighten up release protocols. This issues analysis process is timely and urgent.

7

Sample Chronology: ABC Strategic Planning Workshop

1943 First meeting of deans of our country's medical schools (to discuss physician resources for the war effort—effectively the birth of ABC).

1950s ABC still an informal structure.

1960s Permanent secretariat established, but ABC maintains affiliation with the National Association of Colleges (NAC).

1970s ABC formally established. Office of Research and Information Services (ORIS) established and annual Medical Education Statistics (MES) begins publication.

Committee on Accreditation of Medical Schools (CAMS) formed in partnership with the national medical professional association.

1980s Period of consolidation. Annual meetings held regularly with the Association of Teaching Hospitals (ATH) and eventually the Association for Medical Education (AME); attendance 200.

1990s The National Intern Matching Service (NIMS) becomes the National Residency Matching Service (NRMS) and incorporates independently.

First of still-continuing cooperative ventures with federal government (HIV/AIDS project).

National Medical Forum established with eight other partners.

2000s ATH changes its name to Association of National Academic Healthcare Organizations (ANAHO) and it establishes permanent secretariat; withdraws from participation in Annual Meeting.

Country gets its first new medical school since 1970s—the Island School of Medicine.

Social accountability agenda expands exponentially.

XYZ becomes our formal name in all official languages with a new logo and a new masthead.

XYZ hosts a first-time national conference on medical education (coinciding with its annual meeting) with five national medical co-hosts.

Currently (MM/YY) Facilitated strategic planning.

Change in executive leadership due to retirement of current CEO.

7

PROPOSITIONS

30. The reality in which a process is embedded is always more complex than the words we use to describe it.

31. Self-interest—whether in individuals or groups—may or may not be helpful. It is always complex and easy to misinterpret.

32. Focus on understanding multiple realities. There is no single answer to describe what is happening or what is true.

33. Time invested up front in understanding a situation pays off later when difficulties may arise.

7

8 Developing a Focus

This section in a PTR describes four main aspects of an initiative:

- *Purpose:* A high-level, strategic, and concise description of the reason for the initiative.

- *Objectives:* More specific results that you want to achieve in support of the purpose.

- *Outputs:* What you can achieve or produce during or immediately following a process; outputs are often expressed in numbers.

- *Outcomes:* Short-term outcomes are results that happen soon after a process; medium-term outcomes describe changes in wider settings beyond the direct participants; long-term outcomes are statements of a preferred future for wider settings and take much more time to achieve.

An effective focus section is a clear, engaging, and exact description of what you intend to do in a process. As such, it is an essential requirement for designing and facilitating a process and supporting intended deliverables. It is also closely tied to core assumptions (discussed in Chapter Ten): both sections help you manage expectations, support transparent communication, and ensure that the boundaries and intentions of an initiative don't expand or drift off course.

PURPOSE

The purpose statement describes the fundamental or big-picture reason for a process, for example, "to develop a strategic plan." Process consultants can help clients develop a purpose statement by asking them about the "big question" they want this process to address.

Sometimes a client is clear about the big question underlying a process. For example, "This team is filled with extremely well-educated, often brilliant, and mostly difficult personalities. There is way too much conflict. People need to learn to work together better. The big question is how to make that happen. One vehicle we could use to do this is project planning as it's an important priority now."

Other times clients may know intuitively that a group needs to get together and discuss issues but are not clear about priorities: "We are not meeting our targets, and I'm not sure why; people seem to work together well for the most part but just don't produce." In these situations, the role of the facilitator is to ask the client or planning committee about the "big question" they want this process to address. Some examples of big questions:

Given the similarities and differences in our three companies' corporate cultures and standards, what can we do to ensure that we are successful in global joint business initiatives related to cutting-edge security in banking technology?

What can we do to enhance the way the three national accreditation bodies in our profession work together in the interests of our profession and the public?

How can we improve the health of women in our own countries and around the world in relation to heart disease and stroke?

How you build agreement and reach consensus on the purpose for an initiative will set the tone for and influence how future deliberations happen with people around the table. Having a range of stakeholder perspectives involved clarifies reasoning and intentions, and thereby supports the process and helps keep unexpected perspectives from emerging later.

Just as a map is not the actual territory that you will be exploring, so the PTR (including the purpose, objectives, outputs, and outcomes) is not an exact description of what will happen in a process—it just describes what you want to see happen before you actually start working with people. When you facilitate, you are exploring the territory mapped out in the PTR and experiencing all the realities of being on the ground and walking through that territory with a group of people. These realities may include moments of inspiration, focused insights, and rapid progress as well as miscommunication, conflict, and time spent in off-track conversations.

> The symbol is not the thing symbolized; the word is not the thing; the map is not the territory it stands for.
> —Hayakawa, 1990 [1939], p. 19

Purposeful Language

Think about your purpose in terms of both means and ends. Many purpose statements just describe the outcome or end of a process, for example, "to build a more harmonious workplace." If you include the *means* aspect in this big question (How can we build a more harmonious workplace *through a collaborative approach to planning?*), the purpose is more comprehensive and can help to accelerate and steer the process in a specific direction. The formal task and outcome may be to develop a strategic plan; the issue at the heart of the process is to develop and nurture more harmonious relationships through shared goals and actions.

8

Many purpose statements combine several reasons for a process. Here are examples to illustrate this:

- *Team development, performance management, and leadership development:* To consolidate our corporation's senior management group as a dynamic and well-functioning team, providing coordinated and consistent performance leadership for all employees.

- *Process improvement, best practices, and strategy development:* To continue to work toward fulfilling our future scenario on process improvement by providing an opportunity for partner associations to assess the current state of practice and propose strategies to enhance it over the coming years.

- *Consultation and team development:* To provide an open forum where senior managers can consult with one another in a candid and caring environment on how to address performance management challenges related to fulfilling quarterly targets.

- *Leadership development, issues analysis, and management policy development:* To develop a leadership position and management policies for our organization in relation to current issues affecting clean groundwater in rural environments in our state.

- *Planning, strategy development, and research priority setting:* To develop a national, integrative strategic research agenda among groups and organizations involved in circulatory and respiratory health research, with a focus on scientific excellence in areas of greatest need and opportunity.

Use the following list of possible purpose words to develop purpose statements for a process:

Accountability	Consultation
After-action review	Creative thinking
Best practices	Enabling others (for example, development of regional associations)
Board development	
Building a community of practice	Ethical practices review
Coaching	Evaluation, feedback, review
Communication	Future search

Governance

Information sharing

Innovation for excellence

Issues analysis and management

Knowledge translation (for example, moving research results into practice)

Leadership development

Learning, mentoring

Networking (local, regional, national, global)

Operational implementation

Performance management or improvement

Planning (strategic, operational, goal setting, functional, account)

Policy analysis and development

Priority setting

Problem solving

Process improvement

Performance management

Recommendations review

Report writing

Research (participative, qualitative, quantitative, evidence-informed)

Strategy development

Structure development

Surveillance

Team or group development

Training and development

Values clarification and adoption

Visioning

SAMPLE QUESTIONS FOR DEVELOPING A PURPOSE STATEMENT

At its most basic and fundamental level, what is this process really about?

How will this process contribute significantly to the big-picture goals of your organization? Think in terms of your mission and values.

How would you classify this process? For example, is it about planning and team development? Best practices for accountability and responsibility? National networking? Learning about a specific topic?

> Clients often expect too much or too little from a process. Sometimes we ask a client if it is worthwhile to bring everyone together when the objectives don't seem demanding enough. Other times we are amazed at what people think a group can accomplish in a single day.

8

If you had the power to change the overall situation in your department with respect to achieving quarterly goals, what would you do?

Imagine that it is six months to a year from now, and this problem is solved. What is the most significant change that you can see?

What is the most significant improvement—the biggest win—you would like to see as a result of this process?

What is the one thing you want out of this session that would have a substantive positive impact on your team?

What result would make you feel happiest at the end of this process?

OBJECTIVES, OUTPUTS, AND OUTCOMES

Objectives, outputs, and outcomes have many definitions, which often overlap with and are used interchangeably with terms such as goals, strategic directions, results, priorities, and areas of emphasis. For example, some organizations say that goals and objectives should be SMART: specific, measurable, achievable, relevant, and timely. The SMART acronym is widely used, but often with different words to represent the letters, for example: *strategic* instead of *specific*, *attainable* instead of *achievable*, *resourced* instead of *relevant* (ChangingMinds.org, 2007).

Regardless of how objectives are defined, what is essential is the existence of an agreed-upon definition and a clear and shared understanding among stakeholders of how the objectives will result in intended outputs and outcomes.

Whenever possible, use the language of your client and stakeholders to frame discussions. For example, if they say "strategic direction" and you are accustomed to saying "strategic priority" for the same thing, go with whatever makes people feel comfortable and works for them.

Objectives

In this book, *process objectives* are broad, high-level, measurable action statements that are clearly related to an organization's mission, vision, values, and strategic plan, or those of its stakeholders. Objectives are also designed to fulfill stakeholder expectations.

8

Checklist for objectives:

- Do they describe clearly what the process is going to accomplish?
- Do they help to bridge the gap between your current situation and your anticipated results?
- Do they enable buy-in from key stakeholders?
- Do they support the mission, vision, and core values of participating organizations?
- Do they provide a realistic stretch—that is, are you planning for success that is achievable with some effort, and not calling for something that is unlikely to happen given your current resources?

The objectives for a process flow out of the purpose statement, expanding and clarifying the specifics of what you want to achieve in support of the purpose. They provide a sturdy starting point for an initiative, a strong sense of direction, and usually evolve as participant interactions result in insights and new perspectives about where a process needs to go. These developments may also result in refinements to objectives partway through a process. Be prepared to be flexible and responsive without letting the process run away from you.

Realistic objectives are formulated about real issues. A "presenting issue" is just that: something that seems to be an issue but is often a symptom or sign of an underlying problem that is more significant. Often, initial meetings with clients about designing and facilitating a process begin with clients putting their best foot forward and leaving their worst foot behind, even though process consultants tend to find the more complicated feet the most interesting. Take the time to ask about and listen for the intuitions, assumptions, inconsistencies, or feelings of unease that may signify the need to look more carefully for the real issue.

Well-drawn objectives provide a *realistic stretch*: they push people to do the best they can do (and a little bit more!) within a do-able time frame. Too many objectives are unachievable and reflect the overenthusiasm of planning committee members. Although overambitious objectives may start out in optimism, they usually end up being plans for failure.

8

Learning Objectives

In addition to the formal purpose and objectives, clarify learning objectives, both for participants as individuals and for their organizations. Engage participants in thinking about what they want to learn and how they could take ownership for achieving these objectives through the process.

> Organizations learn only through individuals who learn. Individual learning does not guarantee organizational learning. But without it no organizational learning occurs.
> —Senge, 1990, p. 140.

When writing learning objectives, focus on what the participant, team, or organization will learn rather than on what will be taught.

Individual learning goals don't always line up perfectly with process objectives. Legitimize personal learning goals by confirming their presence. For example, you can say, "An important benefit of these types of sessions is the opportunity to engage in meaningful conversations with fascinating people within a few minutes of meeting them. Take some time to think about what you might like to learn from others in the room and then make the moves to ensure this happens."

Outputs and Outcomes

In process design, the outputs and outcomes are attached to the objectives for the process. They describe in specific terms how a process fits into a larger context by expressing expectations that drive toward immediate, short-term, medium-term, and long-term results.

Outputs are things that you achieve or produce, and you can usually count them. Examples include a report, a change in policy, the number of participants engaged, or the development of specific conclusions or recommendations.

> During a process, the group functions as a temporary, time-limited organization. How can you ensure that it is a *learning* organization for all involved?

Outcomes are direct changes or impacts that are anticipated as a result of a process. Short-term outcome statements are qualitative descriptions of changes in awareness, knowledge, skills, attitudes,

8

or behavior among process participants. Medium-term outcomes flow from short-term outcomes; their statements are qualitative descriptions of key changes in wider settings (such as organizations, neighborhoods, families) beyond the direct participants and after the completion of a process. Long-term outcome statements describe a preferred future for wider settings such as societies, districts, regions, communities, professions.

In process design, objectives, outputs, and outcomes can be mapped as a results chain in a logic model (Figure 8.1).

Clarify expectations regarding outputs and outcomes:

- Will the process be consultative, resulting in input?

- Will it be advisory, resulting in suggestions?

- Will it be decision-focused, resulting in agreement on specified action?

- Will you be developing recommendations? Why or why not? If yes, to whom will recommendations be addressed?

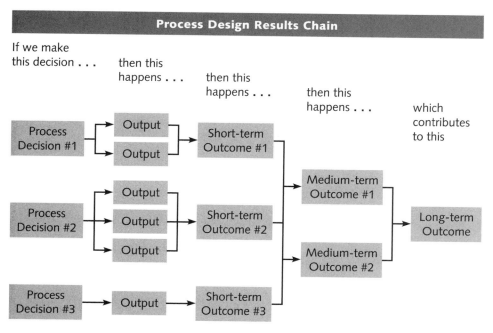

Figure 8.1. Process Design Results Chain
Adapted from Adkins, 2004, p. 33.

8

Sometimes a process will conclude after an output, leaving people in the field to take the next steps related to outcomes. Other times it will conclude after the short-term outcomes have been achieved, and then stakeholders or others will get engaged to move into medium- and longer-term aspects. Make these distinctions and boundaries clear at the outset to avoid misunderstandings about next steps.

SAMPLE QUESTIONS FOR DEVELOPING OBJECTIVES, OUTPUTS, AND OUTCOMES

At what point in the results chain will this process be over? Given that the big question for this initiative is [state here], what subquestions do we need to address in our objectives to support this purpose?

How do the outcomes of this project contribute to our success as a department?

If you could change one key thing as a result of this process, what would you choose and why?

What are the top two issues that this initiative must address? What "undiscussables" (if any) also need to be put on the table?

What common objectives do our partners have that we could support through this initiative?

What current successes, anxieties, or tensions are stakeholders experiencing that would drive people to participate in this process and that you can address through your objectives?

What does the ideal report on this process contain that will serve you well over the next two years?

What outputs (shorter-term) and outcomes (longer-term) would make this process an unqualified success in the eyes of your stakeholders?

What would you like to be different as a result of this process?

When we have achieved this objective, what will others in this group notice (over the shorter term and the longer term) about what has changed or how we are behaving differently?

Where are we most successful and productive in this area? Where are we least successful and productive in this area?

8

PRACTICE GUIDELINES: PURPOSE, OBJECTIVES, OUTPUTS, AND OUTCOMES

Each section of a PTR is interrelated with every other section. For example, the assumptions and key consideration sections need to fit with and supplement discussions about the purpose and objectives. Or if you are designing a process to do strategic planning, then your assumption about budget (discussed in Chapter Ten) for the next three years will play a major role in the planning process.

- Review the purpose and objectives from at least three perspectives:
  - What the participants (represented on committees and in workshops) want
  - What the organization (client) and the stakeholder group expect (based on corporate strategic directions)
  - What the external process consultant or internal manager (internal or external) thinks (based on process experience and expertise)
- Check organizational realities when developing the purpose, objectives, and outcomes:
  - Explore whether objectives fit with stakeholder parameters. For example, in some regions, government employees are not permitted to attend events that have objectives focused on information sharing as this is perceived to be an expensive and inefficient use of employee time.
  - Many organizations are more comfortable writing objectives in terms of task-oriented, measurable efficiencies and effectiveness than in relation to other outcomes that can be more difficult to label due to their complexity, such as increased acceptance, perspective changes, or attitudinal and behavioral changes. Ask about less obvious objectives that your client may wish to address.
  - Use the language of your client group to frame your purpose and objectives. If you are working with an informal group of union representatives, use their language to describe what you want to accomplish rather than language that might be used by senior executives.

8

127

- Determine the readiness of your clients and their team to engage in the process. Prompt them regarding various aspects of the PTR:

    - How does this initiative fit with the current priorities of key stakeholders?

    - What has been done (if anything) to prepare staff for their roles in this process?

    - On a scale of 1 to 5, (where 1 is "not ready at all" and 5 is "as ready as they need to be") how would you describe the readiness of this group with respect to this process?

    - What makes you certain that this process can result in the outputs and outcomes we have described?

- Clear and specific outcomes help stakeholders identify what background information is required to support participants in a process to make quality decisions. In some situations this may involve surveys, reports, or complex comparisons, and in others it may be questions for participants to think about prior to attending a session.

- Name the project clearly once you have confirmed the purpose and objectives, and then use that name consistently. When a project becomes known by a writer's or consultant's name (whether internal or external) rather than by its substantive purpose, then ownership for the initiative can become confused—is this the Jane Smith project or is it the ABC organization's construction project? When stakeholders choose a name that represents and encompasses their collaboration, they begin to own the project and identify with its potential for success.

- You can still create a dynamic and motivating vision while keeping realistic limits in mind. If you aren't realistic, you are planning to fail.

In summary, focus on building ownership for the process purpose and objectives, outputs, and outcomes. Take the time required to explore and clarify each of these areas carefully, ensuring that you have consensus among key stakeholders. If you hear, "What exactly does that mean?" or you sense confusion, focus on what is unclear and put it in plain language, using words that pinpoint the practical realities of the situation.

8

EXAMPLES: PURPOSE, OBJECTIVES, OUTPUTS, AND OUTCOMES

Training and Development in Facilitation: Regional Agency

The purpose of this process is to establish an internal, learning-centered facilitators' network for our region's public services. This network will focus on awareness-raising, skill-development, and networking opportunities for internal facilitators who have an interest in volunteer facilitation over the next few years.

Objectives:

1. To launch our facilitators' network.

   Output: Engage 250 participants in a region-wide explanatory and motivational town hall meeting and distribute information about the network to them.

   Short-term outcome: Participants identify with the network and others using it; they start using the name in short form ("The Network") in conversations with colleagues, and they distribute promotional packages to three potential new members.

   Medium-term outcome: Facilitators will be comfortable using a virtual facilitators Web site to link with, share information with, and learn from other employees; a comprehensive database will be in place to support interaction among employees.

   Long-term outcome: Trained volunteer facilitators will be available, confident about their facilitation skills, and interested in facilitating future public participation initiatives. The virtual network will enable regular regional learning opportunities designed specifically for internal facilitators.

2. To support skill development through information sharing and experiential, learning-centered training and development.

   Output: Participants (250) will receive copies of three facilitation handbooks and participate in two active learning experiences of their choice, integrating new tools and skills in their facilitation practice.

   Short-term outcome: Participants will use the facilitation manuals as desktop resources to support both formal and ongoing day-to-day informal facilitation experiences in the workplace.

(continued on next page)

8

Training and Development in Facilitation: Regional Agency, Cont'd.

Medium-term outcome: Participation in training sessions and later engagement as facilitators will contribute to confidence building in facilitation.

Long-term outcome: The region will have the facilitation resources required to fulfill consultation objectives over the next five years.

3. To recognize the contribution and efforts of volunteer facilitators in support of the regional governments' public participation initiatives.

Output: The administrator will report on the results of the recent two public consultations on budget priorities and on postsecondary education, acknowledging positive evaluation results. Public service awards will be provided to section heads who organized volunteer facilitators for exceptional contributions under difficult timelines.

Short-term outcome: Volunteer facilitators will appreciate formal acknowledgment of their efforts, and senior officials will recognize the important contribution of facilitation to effective consultations with the public.

Long-term outcome: Facilitators will expand their network to include process design as part of their repertoire of skills.

International Congress: Infectious Disease Control

The purpose of the 4th International Infectious Disease Control Congress is to provide an opportunity for a broad constituency of global stakeholders involved in infectious disease control to work together and learn from one another.

Objectives

1. To provide an opportunity for mutual learning and knowledge transfer among countries with existing infectious disease control strategies and countries with strategies under development, while recognizing unique challenges and supports among health delivery systems.

Output: Engagement of 175 country representatives in a four-day learning opportunity; a report on key learnings and conclusions for distribution to participants and other stakeholders.

8

International Congress: Infectious Disease Control, Cont'd.

Short-term outcome: New connections among representatives from countries with related concerns and opportunities.

Medium-term outcome: Greater understanding of and mutual support for addressing common and unique challenges in infectious disease control at a global level.

Long-term outcome: Increased regular networking and collaboration among a range of countries, national organizations, and individuals with an interest in population-based national infectious disease control.

2. To learn about and develop conclusions in four key areas of the spectrum of infectious disease control:

   a. WHY. The science underlying infectious disease control: What is the evidence for the effectiveness of population-based approaches to infectious disease control that drives the need for national control programs?

   b. WHAT. The content of infectious disease control: What are the programmatic activities of infectious disease control? What are the measures (process, quality, and outcome) of success? What additional quality programs and measurements are required for future success?

   c. HOW. The organization of national infectious disease control: How can we develop national infectious disease control strategies to support maximum impact?

   d. WHO. Participation in infectious disease control: Who should be at national tables to optimize the success of population-based infectious disease control programs?

   Output: Answers to the four basic questions in the form of conclusions for future infectious disease control programs.

   Medium-term outcome: A report providing global comparisons of responses to these four questions.

3. To develop a virtual community of practice where international stakeholders such as the Global Health Group (GHG), the International Alliance For Infectious Disease Control (IAIDC), and interested countries and organizations can share information and learn together based on shared challenges.

(continued on next page)

8

131

International Congress: Infectious Disease Control, Cont'd.

In this context, a community of practice becomes an engine driving enhanced global infectious disease control.

Output: Demonstration of global, national, and local virtual communities of practice during the Congress.

Short-term outcome: Experimentation with new software as a viable research mechanism in interested countries.

Medium-term outcome: Increased regular international collaboration and dialogue among countries with infectious disease control plans and those interested in developing such plans; a shared sense of mutual obligation among participants; a mechanism to support an active international community of practice in infectious disease control.

Long-term outcome: Commitment in theory and practice to demonstrated benefits of virtual communities of practice.

4. To learn about the latest science of population-based infectious disease control and identify gaps for an international strategic research agenda for infectious disease control.

Output: A report with conclusions about strategic research gaps.

Short-term outcome: Meeting of interested researchers immediately following the forum to explore opportunities for developing a research community of practice.

Medium-term outcome: International research collaborations focused on agreed strategic research gaps.

5. To facilitate international networking during the Congress among individuals involved in all aspects of infectious disease control.

Output: Establishment of new relationships and support for existing relationships to benefit infectious disease control.

PROPOSITIONS

34. The client, sponsor, and stakeholders are accountable for ensuring that the ends are appropriate. The process designer is accountable for ensuring that the means to achieve the ends are appropriate.

35. Means-ends gaps and inconsistencies in the purpose, objectives, outputs, and outcomes reflect a lack of critical reflection and consensus building among stakeholders.

36. Transparency in rationale, expectations, and intentions must be a byword to support a robust and efficient process.

37. Silence does not mean consent.

38. Organizations learn more through issues-based, collaborative, consensus-building processes than through any other approach.

8

9 Stakeholder Collaboration

Stakeholders are individuals, groups, and organizations with a significant vested interest in the purpose, objectives, and outcomes of a process. Stakeholders are often members of more than one constituency. They may affect or be affected by an initiative's outputs and outcomes, and thus they usually have an interest in oversight, quality, efficiency, and effectiveness.

9

STAKEHOLDER PERSPECTIVES AND CATEGORIES

Although stakeholders are key players in a process, they are not necessarily full participants in all aspects of it, particularly meetings and workshops that focus on specific topics or where resources are limited.

Some stakeholders may contribute to a process through a pre-workshop questionnaire or consultation and not attend a final decision-making event. Others may develop background information for a task force or deliver an expert opinion in a presentation at a seminar; still others may have a role in representing an organization with a strong stake in the results of a process.

Use these general categories to spark some thoughts about who might be stakeholders in a process, keeping in mind that some initiatives have a very small group of stakeholders and others a very large one:

- *Advocates:* opinion leaders, special interest groups, shareholders, funders, unions

- *Authorities:* board members, decision makers, leaders, implementers, shareholders, regulators, sponsors

- *Clients:* initial, intermediate, primary, or ultimate client (Schein, 1987)

- *Content experts:* professional practitioners, specialists, lawyers, ethicists, public policy specialists, researchers (including basic science, applied science, systems and services, societal, cultural, and environmental areas)

- *Customers:* purchasers of the organization's goods or services

- *Established priority groups:* people with disabilities, rural and remote populations, native and ethnocultural groups

- *Members:* voting members, employees, unions

> Connecting to and satisfying stakeholders is a complex task—relationships differ, their weight of influence varies, competing interests must be balanced, and conflicting perspectives reconciled. Obligations can be legal, such as between the organization and its members; practical, such as between the organization and its funders; or moral, such as between the organization and its clients or the public-at-large.
> —Institute on Governance, n.d.

- *Other information sources:* colleagues, competitors, clients, media

- *Public:* citizens, consumers, media, residents, informed members of the lay public who have experience in the issue area

- *Related experts:* people who may not be directly involved but who could provide an innovative perspective, such as hibernation scientists providing input on emergency rescue strategies in very cold climates or for those who have fallen through frozen lake surfaces

- *Representatives:* of organizations and groups; of related boards, governments, and nongovernment organizations (including foundations and charities); of sponsors, unions, and geographical areas such as states and provinces; of educational backgrounds

- *Spiritual advisers:* representatives of established religious groups with an interest in issues related to an initiative

- *People of wisdom:* individuals who have experience in the area and are respected for their abilities in critical reflection

SAMPLE QUESTIONS FOR IDENTIFYING STAKEHOLDERS

How are we defining *key stakeholder* in this initiative?

How are we defining *expertise* in this initiative?

How can we encourage stakeholders to develop ownership for this initiative so that they stay involved after the process is over?

How can we engage groups and sectors that are important to our discussions but often aren't involved? That is, can we hold interviews with (or send questionnaires to) other individuals, organizations, networks, sectors, interest groups?

How can we introduce new perspectives? What are the percentages of new and old stakeholders in this initiative? Is this appropriate or should we be adjusting the balance?

How many people involved in the process will be instrumental in the implementation of recommendations?

How should people be invited? Formally through the leaders of their departments or organizations, or informally at first by individuals who know them well and to whom they may be more receptive?

How, when, and where will stakeholders participate in this process? Who will participate in what aspects (questionnaires, interviews, meetings, workshops)?

What types of power do we want participants to bring to this initiative: expertise, professional affiliation, organizational representation, positional power, specific perspectives, decision-making authority, skills in collaboration, support?

What (if any) are the social responsibility commitments of stakeholder organizations? How might this initiative tie in with those?

What levels, groups, or other units in your organization will be affected by what you are doing in this process? How will you ensure that their perspectives are included?

Who are obvious and less obvious champions of the process and its anticipated outcomes?

Who might be described as "a breath of fresh air" in this process?

Who would be disappointed if they weren't invited to be a part of this process and only heard about it after the fact?

> *Expertise* is a complex concept. Each person's experience, education, background, and perspective contribute to expertise and provide a reference point for discussions throughout a process. The facilitator's role is to enable participants to understand one another's expertise and its relative value within a process.

PRACTICE GUIDELINES: STAKEHOLDER COLLABORATION

Be clear about criteria for stakeholders and use them to decide who should be involved, why, how, and at what point in the process.

- Consider to what extent your stakeholder list is exclusive or inclusive and the potential effect your answer will have on the longer-term impact of this process. Think about the conditions that might exclude people, groups, communities, and populations from participating in processes where they see themselves as stakeholders (Shookner, 2002, pp. 2–5).

- Describe the stakeholder perspectives represented at each session (discussed in Chapter Three). Name these perspectives and how they link to your objectives.

  For each stakeholder group or organization, describe:

  - Mission or purpose and vision or key goals

  - Core values

  - Current challenges that relate to the purpose of this initiative

- Facilitate a transparent discussion about what types of power (discussed in Chapter Four) are needed to support a successful initiative and who can provide it to support the group in achieving anticipated outcomes and long-term change.

- For each stakeholder group or organization do a give-get analysis. Describe:

  - What they could or might want to *contribute to* the process

  - What they might want to *get from* the process

  Do a similar give-get analysis for individuals: name one or two participants who you think can make a substantive contribution to the outputs, and are likely to benefit from and contribute to implementation of the process results.

- Stakeholder descriptions can vary considerably. Ask your client how to describe them appropriately. For example, are they customers, municipal partners, alliance members, co-operants, owners, sponsors?

- For each workshop objective, name one or two participants who you think can make a substantive contribution to achieving that objective, and are likely to benefit from and contribute to implementation of the process results.

- Questions about the appropriateness of observers or participant-observers often come up when discussing stakeholder participants in a process. Clarify what you mean by the terms *observer* or *participant-observer*. Are these individuals not to participate in any way, or in some ways but not others? The more clarity and transparency you bring to this situation, the more comfortable the observers and other participants will be in the workshop.

9

- If an observer is to take notes for a report or in preparation for a summary given in the plenary session, make sure the rest of the group understands that the note-taker is to be objective and not involved in group discussions.

- If a vice president in an organization wants to observe a series of half-day meetings on issues analysis with a group managed by a direct report, what exactly does the VP mean by "observe"? What impact will this attendance have on participants' comfort in disclosing concerns and discussing them openly? How will the direct report feel in this situation?

- A participant-observer role may be requested for staff at an annual board meeting for members of a professional association. In this situation, staff are often not permitted to vote or influence discussion as they are present in their capacity as experts on specific questions. Thus they participate by providing information but observe when it comes to discussion and decision making.

- Develop a matrix that makes obvious the categories and perspectives of participants and which hats they can wear in the initiative (see Figure 9.1). Whether this is an internal or external process, by invitation or through mandatory attendance, it is important to know who is bringing what to the process.

- Set norms for working together with key stakeholders on various committees. Ask stakeholders to name the norms based on how they have been working together: What do we do well in these meetings? What could we focus on more? Encourage everyone to refer to the norms as a way to remind each other about how they have agreed to work together.

- When you look at the group as a whole, what do you think the tone of this process is likely to be? Why do you think this is so? How can you check out your inferences? Is this tone what you think would work best for this initiative?

Potential Invitees			Content Expertise	A. Criteria										B. Affiliation				C. Other	Comments
Last Name	First Name	Organization		Academia	Basic Biomedical	Clinical	Health Systems and Health Services	Societal, Cultural and Environmental Influences	Knowledge Transfer and Capacity-building Expertise	Consumer (and comfortable with the process)	Nongovernmental Organization	Clinicians (physicians, nurses, and so on)	International Representation	Home Location	Gender	Planning Committee Member	Reference Group Member		
1																			
2																			
3																			
4																			
5																			
6																			
7																			
8																			
9																			
10																			
11																			
12																			
13																			
14																			
15																			
16																			
17																			
18																			
19																			
20																			
21																			
22																			
23																			
24																			
25																			

Figure 9.1. Sample Matrix

EXAMPLES: KEY STAKEHOLDERS

9

Strategic Planning Process:
Urban Law Firm with Eighteen Partners

As shareholders in our firm, our partners are our first stakeholders. Our clients are also a top priority as they keep our firm alive and vibrant, and they have a personal stake in our success. Other stakeholders include our state Bar Association and local and regional governments. All our stakeholders bring an interest in high-quality and timely legal services.

Here is how each of these groups will be involved in this process:

- Consulted prior to planning sessions:
  - Partners and clients
  - Expert on new legal regulations and recent regional legal conference reports
  - Local expert on strategic planning in law firms

- Participation in planning sessions:
  - Firm partners
  - Senior staff
  - Keynote speaker representing local legal advocacy group
  - Keynote speaker on current ethical issues for law firms in our region

- Follow-through after participatory sessions:
  - Firm manager
  - Chairs of partner groups

National Forum: Alcohol and Illicit Drugs Research

For the purposes of this process, key stakeholders are individuals, groups, and organizations with a significant vested interest in research into addictions and the use of alcohol and illicit drugs in our country. Stakeholders contribute to this research in a variety of ways, such as funding, developing, conducting, disseminating, and applying research. Stakeholders also bring a variety of interests to this research, including high-quality and appropriate research processes

National Forum: Alcohol and Illicit Drugs Research, Cont'd.

9

and results, evidence-based practices, clear health and social outcomes for people with addictions, collaborative approaches, and accountability.

Here is how stakeholders will be involved in this process:

- Consulted prior to planning sessions:
  - Funders such as research granting agencies and the pharmaceutical industry
  - Epidemiologists to write a discussion paper on the current situation including recent changes in laws
  - The public, through an opinion survey conducted by an objective outside group

- Participation in planning sessions:
  - Expert speakers (national and international)
  - Senior researchers from bench to bedside, including those with integrated interdisciplinary experience
  - Community-based drug addiction specialists such as counselors, mobile crisis intervention units
  - Psychiatrists, psychologists, qualified counselors, and nurse specialists
  - Experts (national and international) in prevention, health promotion, knowledge dissemination, and translation
  - Specialists in gender-related issues and impacts
  - Experienced individuals such as former patients who are working in innovative street programs
  - Representatives of government programs at various levels including senior policymakers
  - Educators of children and youth including school counseling programs

- Knowledge transfer and implementation after planning sessions:
  - Editors of two national journals and one international journal on addictions
  - Federal government policymakers
  - Nongovernment, union, and private sectors sponsors

9

PROPOSITIONS

39. Treating stakeholders as individuals of irreplaceable value is the basis of collaboration.

40. Stakeholders with much power and little commitment are not as valuable as those with less power and a lot of commitment.

41. Visionary stakeholder values that contradict popular expectations probably foreshadow transformation.

42. Charisma is not the basis of facilitative leadership.

10 Core Assumptions

Core assumptions are the agreed-upon givens or decisions that provide a common starting point for reflection, discussion, and decision making. They define the project scope, outline the perspective within which a process unfolds, and help ensure that everyone involved is on the same page—that is, focused on a common purpose and objectives within a shared understanding of the context and anticipated outcomes.

Assumptions are often implicit rather than explicit, and therefore they are not easy to articulate. Because they are also not often discussed, significant benefits accrue when they are stated, clarified, and validated. For example:

- Participants share a common understanding about the basic parameters of a process.

- Contentious issues that aren't and shouldn't be on the agenda are taken off the table by prior agreement.

- "Undiscussables" that need to be explored can be identified up front and moved into the "key considerations" part of the PTR.

- The facilitator can declare up front in a session that the assumptions were developed by people with the authority to make them and therefore the group can simply use them and move on.

It is essential to distinguish between core assumptions and key considerations (discussed in Chapter Eleven). The core assumptions section of a PTR focuses on decisions already made that provide a starting point for a process. The key considerations section is devoted to issues, factors, risks, and opportunities with the potential to influence the design and facilitation of a process and for which decisions have not been made. Key considerations are open for discussion; core assumptions are not.

The core assumptions section in a PTR states the following:

- Scope
- Values and ethical practices that are germane to deliberations and decision making
- Controversial issues and how they will or won't be addressed during a process
- Existing policies and guidelines
- History of the organization
- How this initiative fits into a related strategic plan (mission, vision, strategic directions)

> Validate core assumptions before creating the process design. Keep in mind that *core* refers to the heart of the matter; it means central, principal, primary, fundamental.

- How this initiative fits into a related operational plan (priorities, staff skills, resource allocation)

- Levels of evidence: relevant research, consultations, and facts on which the initiative is based

- Where the results and report of the initiative will go for further consideration (for example, experts who have made themselves available for consultation) or for final decisions (for example, to a board of directors with authority to rule on the issue)

- Approval process for reports

10

SCOPE

The scope of a process describes its focus, parameters, and jurisdiction. Being clear about assumptions related to scope in a PTR prevents issues from arising later on, when a process is gaining momentum. Scope creep (changes in the boundaries or jurisdiction of a project), or scope drift (adjustments in the intention or focus of a project) are common problems in process design that can result in cost overruns, processes with too many objectives, a confusing flow, an uncertain sense of direction, and too much work to do in not enough time.

Creep

Scope creep usually happens because the client, executive sponsor, and process consultant are not clear about project boundaries with colleagues or other stakeholders. It may be intentional or unintentional. Scope creep may emerge as pressure from a colleague: "I think it's great that you've started this process. And it just so happens that it ties in perfectly with something that we've been thinking about doing for some time now. How about if we include our issue with yours and tackle them both using the same process?" If no one is keeping a close watch on the project scope, it can quickly become unmanageable as it expands beyond its intended boundaries.

Think carefully about the amount of time, energy, and other resources you have available to do a process before agreeing to changes in scope. Your response

10

to the suggestion in the preceding paragraph might be: "Let's go back to the PTR and review where we started with all this. At that time you were clear about the purpose and objectives and that this initiative would take six months of extensive research, meetings, workshops, reports, and communication. You also said that it was important that the

> In Jeet Kune Do, one does not accumulate but eliminate. It is not daily increase but daily decrease. The height of cultivation always runs to simplicity.
> —Bruce Lee

item we are discussing now was off the table for this initiative. What has changed since then to convince you that it should be on the table now?"

Drift

Scope drift usually happens slowly and often imperceptibly. As stakeholders become engaged and enthusiastic about an initiative, the initial focus somehow seems to slip sideways and evolve into a similar but different project. You're still going in the same general direction but you've lost your specific focus. When scope drift is noticed, people often comment that they weren't aware that they had lost direction. This noticing is the first step for discussions that can get the process back on track.

SAMPLE QUESTIONS FOR DEVELOPING ASSUMPTIONS

Given the inputs or resources we have for this initiative and what you know about the context, what is on and off the table (that is, included and excluded) with respect to this process?

How, when, and by whom will decisions be made? What decisions have already been made?

In general, how will implementation happen after this process is complete?

What (if anything) is nonnegotiable in this process? Why is it nonnegotiable?

What are we assuming about the current social and political climate with respect to this initiative?

What aspects of this initiative are outside our control?

What assumptions or first premises are there in how we are going about this process that we may be taking for granted and that others may not regard as so certain?

What group norms (such as candor, tact, active listening) will guide how we work together on this initiative?

What is our authority, jurisdiction, or influence with respect to implementing the results of this initiative? or What is our intended reach in terms of impact for this project?

What official positions, policies, codes, or laws apply to this process? Are there any organizational by-laws, rules, guidelines, or policies that should be stated as assumptions to guide this initiative?

What potential conflicts of interest (trust issues) and congruencies of interest (parallel intentions) do we need to name up front?

What values in our organization, sector, or society are most important to demonstrate in this process?

Which key terms do we need to be clear about due to implications for this initiative (for example, *client, safe practice, manageable risk, advisory*)?

> To reach a port we must sail, sometimes with the wind, and sometimes against it. But we must not drift or lie at anchor.
> —Oliver Wendell Holmes

PRACTICE GUIDELINES: CORE ASSUMPTIONS

- Ensure that key stakeholders understand and agree with the scope of the initiative. If they don't agree, discuss and come to agreement on scope before proceeding. Be specific about parameters. For example, "We will not be discussing any aspect of project management at this retreat. Our focus will be strategic."

- Scope is often implicit in the purpose and objectives. Decide which aspects of your process require an explicit statement about scope (for example, when competing interests may be nervous about the possibility of an initiative stepping on their toes). Encourage transparency about intentions and interests from the get-go.

- Ask the Process Planning Committee members what assumptions are required to encompass the context and the range of perspectives at the table throughout the process. Consider several types of assumptions depending on whether they are based on:

  - WHAT: corporate goals
  - HOW: norms for working together
  - WHO: participants in various parts of a process
  - WHEN: time lines for the main parts of a process
  - WHY: a rationale for why things are done the way they are
  - WHERE: location of boundary disputes

  While discussing a core assumption, you may discover that it should really be a key consideration, that is, open for discussion in a process.

- Check that you have agreement among stakeholders on each assumption before including it in a PTR. Use clear, specific language and a direct question to confirm agreement. Invalid, untested assumptions lead to invalid, untested decisions that aren't grounded in stakeholders' realities.

- Ensure that you have the right degree of specificity in your assumptions. Some assumptions need to be quite detailed (for example, for the development of forestry practice guidelines or who will be involved after an initiative is completed), while others can be more general (for example, about the current political climate).

- Ensure that your assumptions address potential yes-but situations in a process. For example, if you don't want discussions about resources to sidetrack decision making with comments such as "yes, but this isn't realistic given resources," then you can take that topic off the table in this section to prevent that discussion from arising. A sample assumption in this situation might be, "For the purposes of this process, resources are assumed to be the same as last year plus 10 percent."

- Include an assumption about decision making that clarifies which participants in a process are advisory and which ones will make decisions. For example, will final decisions be made during a workshop or afterward, perhaps by a senior administrator, an expert panel, or a board of directors?

- Create baseline assumptions when there are differences in belief and no authoritative or commonly accepted fact to anchor discussion. For example, stakeholders may develop an assumption that states that they are concerned about the lack of international policy to guide shared boundary disputes about water resources even though there is currently not enough science to support the development of that policy.

- Test stakeholders' assumptions about the best type of process for an initiative. For example, if you make the assumption that the right people are in the room to do the work and you are missing key perspectives, commitments, or types of power, this may affect your ability to achieve meaningful outcomes over the longer term.

- Once the core assumptions are in draft form, check them against the purpose and objectives:

  - Which assumptions have the potential to have an impact on which objectives?

  - To what extent will each assumption influence the degree to which that objective can be achieved?

EXAMPLES: CORE ASSUMPTIONS

Pan-Country Forum: Alcohol and Illicit Drugs Research

It is essential to get a wide range of perspectives on this initiative to support intelligent decision making. Participants should include researchers from a range of disciplines, policy developers, decision makers, clinician scientists, practitioners, service deliverers, community workers, and informed members of the public.

Current research efforts in North America are hampered by the absence of a coordinated approach. While some preliminary work has been done to build a strategic research agenda and strengthen collaboration among

---

(continued on next page)

10

Pan-Country Forum: Alcohol and Illicit Drugs Research, Cont'd.

---

stakeholders within this field and between the field and funding bodies, there is a continuing need to promote multidisciplinary approaches that cross all types of research.

One result of this Forum will be a large, collaborative, multicountry, multidisciplinary research initiative. Based on recent government announcements, it is safe to assume that the economic, social, and political climate in North America is supportive of a collaborative research project like this one.

Funding for research into addictions and the use of alcohol and illicit drugs has become increasingly sporadic in recent years. As a result, the sharing of knowledge among the many disciplines and jurisdictions involved in this area has suffered.

Socially and economically disadvantaged groups (including unemployed, underemployed, street youth and women) are particularly vulnerable to the effects of addiction.

Forum participants are committed to taking the results of the Forum to their professional organizations and communities of interest for discussion and action.

Note the differences between the assumptions developed for this case and those for the next one.

Creating a Tool for Collaboration in Policy Development

The following five assumptions are the basis for developing a guide on how to use a collaborative approach to develop health policy (Tomlinson and Strachan, 2005, pp. 2–5). These assumptions were developed by a national steering committee and confirmed (along with draft versions of the guide) through a two-year needs assessment and multi-workshop process with hundreds of participants in the public and nonprofit sectors.

- Developing health policy collaboratively begins with a commitment to mutual respect, inclusiveness, accessibility, clarity, transparency, responsibility and accountability (Voluntary Sector Initiative: Canada, 2002, pp. 6–7).

Creating a Tool for Collaboration in Policy Development, Cont'd.

- Policy development is complex and variable. There is no one best way to develop policy or to collaborate; each initiative is fundamentally unique. As a result, those involved need to
  - Learn from experience, both their own and those of others.
  - Develop common understandings based on shared experiences.
  - Manage individual personalities.
  - Understand the ins and outs of specific policies and policy development processes.
  - Adapt to current and changing conditions, including available resources.
- Collaboration engages stakeholders in a distinct set of processes, that is, a continuing series of actions, events, and changes. Everyone who has worked collaboratively has experienced various aspects of these processes. Collaborators are often aware that these processes are occurring, but they don't usually think about them in an organized way.
- The "what" and "how" of collaborative policy development are distinct perspectives. This guide focuses on how to work with others when developing policies, that is, the interactive processes involved in collaboration.
- A range of excellent resources on the "what" of policy development already exists. The purpose of this initiative is not to duplicate these resources.

10

PROPOSITIONS

43. Assumptions make the implicit explicit. This is a good thing.

44. When assumptions are unclear, they can jump up and bite you when you're in the middle of a process. This is a bad thing.

45. Scope drift and creep are symptoms of underlying problems related to inaccurate or unowned purpose, objectives, and outcomes.

46. Assumptions in a PTR can address potential yes-buts in a group discussion.

11 Key Considerations

Every process has important circumstances, data, reflections, and concerns that need to be taken into account because of their potential impact on the success of the initiative. When these considerations are noted in a PTR, they can be kept at the forefront of deliberations, explored with possible consequences in mind, and revisited by the facilitator and participants as required.

When noting key considerations, think about potential impacts related to key decisions in a process. The idea is to select significant impacts rather than to include every item that comes up.

The key considerations section in a PTR states the following:

- Major risks and opportunities embedded in the process
- The potential impact of related initiatives
- Significant internal and external pressures
- PEST: political-legal, economic, sociocultural, and technological factors and trends (see www.marketingteacher.com/Lessons)
- Current state of relationships among key players
- Time frames: what makes this initiative timely, urgent, essential; completion time lines
- Potential implementation challenges
- Data essential to making informed decisions in key result areas
- How the outputs and outcomes of the initiative will be evaluated

> One thinks of Wittgenstein's image of a man in the street viewed from behind a closed window. He appears to be walking upright but in truth he may be in highly unstable equilibrium, barely balancing against the gale of wind he is leaning into: Generally it is what is *not* seen that matters.
>   —Hodgkinson, 1996, pp. 152–153

Although core assumptions and key considerations are distinct entities, deciding whether an item should be included in one area or the other can be confusing. Figure 11.1 outlines some suggestions to help distinguish between these two essential aspects of a PTR.

Ultimately, the decision about whether an item is an assumption or a key consideration depends on the will of the planning committee for a process.

SAMPLE QUESTIONS FOR DEVELOPING KEY CONSIDERATIONS

Are the presenting issues (defined in Chapter Three) the real issues or are there "undiscussables" that are also important potential opportunities or challenges that need to be put on our table?

11

Core Assumptions	Key Considerations
The basic givens or initial decisions on which a process is based. Example: Funding is fixed over the next twelve months.	Important issues that must be considered throughout a process. Example: Funding for the next twelve months is in jeopardy.
Once confirmed by individuals with positional authority such as process planning committee members, these are not open for discussion except in unusual circumstances.	Once confirmed by individuals with positional authority such as process planning committee members, these become important items for further discussion and decision making in terms of their potential impact on a process.
Decisions have been made and are off the table throughout the process.	Issues have been identified and are on the table throughout the process.
When they surface in discussions, facilitator reminds stakeholders that these items have been discussed and decided by planning committee members as part of determining the scope of the initiative, and they are not open for deliberation.	When they surface in discussions, facilitator may wish to remind stakeholders that these items have been identified as potentially having a considerable impact (positive or negative) on process outputs and outcomes.

Figure 11.1. Assumptions and Considerations

From your perspective, is there a prevailing attitude toward this initiative? Please explain.

How do you want to represent intended and unintended potential consequences with respect to related initiatives?

Processes usually take place in a sea of related initiatives. From your perspective, what is happening at provincial or state, regional, national, and international levels in relation to your organization's interests that should be taken into consideration during this planning process?

To what extent are the client and stakeholders part of the problem? Part of the solution?

What are your [partners, competitors, colleagues, sister organizations, suppliers, collaborators, funders, professional associations, unions, and so on] doing that is related to or could have an impact on this process?

What are the implications of this process for other initiatives in which your organization is involved or has a stake?

What are the potential big "P" and small "p" politics that can affect the success of this initiative?

What is at stake here with respect to this process?

What is currently going on (or has happened recently) that could have an impact on the nature and success of this process?

What is the capacity of the organizations involved in this initiative (for example, with respect to administration, committee membership, expertise, money for this initiative)? How can the range of capacities have an impact on involvement and stakeholder relationships?

What is the evidence of need for this process?

What key considerations (internal) related to McKinsey's original 7S's framework (Strategy, Structure, Systems, Staff, Style, Shared values, Skills) do we need to consider for this process to be successful? (www.mckinsey.com)

What key considerations (external) related to the PEST framework (political-legal, economic, sociocultural, and technological factors) do we need to consider for this process to be successful? (See www.marketingteacher.com/Lessons.)

What other work is going on in this area in your organization? Could this process support or duplicate work that others have done or are doing?

What recent reports and publications are you aware of that relate to this initiative?

Where is the organization most successful and productive in this area? Where is it least successful and productive in this area?

Will you recommend someone who has a different perspective or opinion on this whom I could speak with?

PRACTICE GUIDELINES: KEY CONSIDERATIONS

The successful management of key considerations depends on the resourcefulness, flexibility, and commitment of individuals in a process to work within a frequently changing dynamic. Examples of key considerations include potential changes of government, fluctuations in commodity prices, lack of evidence to support decision making, political dynamics that affect the future of a project, and the evolving nature of commitments by key stakeholders.

> Key considerations are items with the potential to unsettle a process if not identified and addressed in a timely fashion.

11

- Once the key considerations are in draft form, check them against the purpose and objectives:
  - Which considerations have the potential to have an impact on which objectives?
  - To what extent will each consideration influence the degree to which that objective can be achieved?
- Describe succinctly (in two or three sentences) the values tensions in the process and how they might be related to key considerations. Then check out your conclusions with clients and stakeholders. For example:
  - Does the primary client value the initiative to a much greater extent than the participants do?
  - Are there values tensions between stakeholder groups that are treated as undiscussables?
  - Which preference-level values are at play in individuals? For example, how do people feel about the location, the food, the chairs?
  - Do values tensions exist between stakeholder groups?
  - What undiscussables about values conflicts need to be raised?
- Identify where the tensions or conflicts are located:
  - Within individuals?
  - Between stakeholder or other subgroups, both formal and informal?

- - Between authority levels within stakeholder organizations—that is, among employees, between management and employees, between senior and middle management, or between the board and senior managers?

  - Within the wider related community?

- Naming a key consideration is an important step: pick your words carefully. For example, the more generic language of "family violence" evokes different reactions and means something different from the specific terminology of "spouse assault."

- When checking the wording in a key consideration, ask yourself whether a special interest group with a stake in that key consideration would find your wording accurate, meaningful, and appropriate.

- Explore ethical considerations in relation to stakeholder groups and how these may affect conflicts of interest regarding stakeholder participation; for example, the involvement of private sector corporations in processes to determine strategic priorities of publicly funded systems such as environmental protection or prescription drugs, or the active participation of board members who can influence legal parameters for mergers in which they have a financial stake.

- Be aware that while discussing a key consideration you may discover that it should really be a core assumption or a given in a process.

EXAMPLES: KEY CONSIDERATIONS

Regional Account Planning: Technology Sector

a. We have a great sales team: people are competent; they do well financially; they share tips, build on each other's accomplishments, and usually enjoy each other's company.

b. Our corporation is losing market share to smaller, faster-moving companies who can be more nimble in responding to client needs.

Regional Account Planning: Technology Sector, Cont'd.

c. Governments are asking for more demonstration units: this is cutting into our profit margin.

d. The entire technology sector is still suffering badly from the dot-com crash and the outlook for another few years isn't bright.

e. The military budget has been overspent and the technology side is experiencing drastic cuts. This is reflected in our loss of market share in this area.

f. We have lost one senior account manager to illness and another to a competitor in the past six months; morale is low.

g. Our new Web-based software product for corporate security is fast, sexy, easy to use, and makes a big positive initial impression when demonstrated. Last month's sales were 10 percent higher than predictions.

h. The unexpected financial problems of our top two competitors provide us with a significant but limited window of opportunity for increasing market share.

i. Resources are questionable; no new funds will be available for the next twelve months.

11

Strategic Planning Process: Urban Law Firm with Eighteen Partners

a. The two partners who left ten months ago and started their own firm are already doing well in the family practice area, and we are hearing about their success informally. Although we no longer have a family practice area, this inevitably hurts us, not just in terms of reputation but with respect to referrals.

b. Our clients are better informed than ever. Many of them come into our offices with a preliminary strategy worked out, and they are quite comfortable using legal terminology. Because they are doing research on the Web, they are also more comfortable challenging our fees and how much time it takes us to complete specific types of work.

(continued on next page)

11

Strategic Planning Process:
Urban Law Firm with Eighteen Partners, Cont'd.

---

c. Lifelong loyalty to a single firm is changing as clients are prepared to shop around for what they want. They also want service when they need it; the old days of 9–5 hours are rapidly disappearing.

d. Large firms are getting larger: we have had two invitations to join firms in our state capital.

e. It is no longer necessary to be physically present to offer clients top-notch service.

f. The management of law firms is changing constantly and we need to explore whether we should be trying to be more efficient. In the past it was assumed that a senior partner would take on the responsibility for ongoing management. Today professional managers with no experience in law are running many high-profile firms. This change has prompted a review of operational systems, payment expectations, and strategies, as well as a rethinking of values.

g. Comprehensive firms that offer accounting, legal, and process expertise are moving away from our traditional siloed approach to the law. One-stop shopping is appealing to customers, and if they can't get it from us they will go somewhere else. We need to move these services in-house.

h. Lawyers are looking different and acting differently these days. Many of us are young, female, and of various ethnic and racial origins, and we bring a wide range of perspectives to the firm, including different ways of viewing the practice of law. Articling students aren't always interested in putting in the time to become partners; many of them want a fair salary for a fair day's work so that they can enjoy their families and weekends. This was unheard of even five years ago.

i. Most partners and legal assistants are working more, making less, and spending less time with their families. This results in increased pressures on several fronts. A number of partners have commented on the less-than-optimal interpersonal climate in the office over the past year.

Strategic Planning Process:
Urban Law Firm with Eighteen Partners, Cont'd.

---

j. An election is coming up and it looks as if we will be losing some of our key contacts and sources of work in the legislature.

k. Most states have more lawyers than required to do the amount of work available. Addressing this fact requires involvement in policy development at the state level and a commitment to a value-added approach to service that could significantly reduce revenues.

11

PROPOSITIONS

47. The ability of a group to clarify key considerations is directly related to the degree to which transparency is operative among individual group members.

48. What is an assumption for one client group may be a key consideration for another: it depends on whether the item is on or off the table.

49. Insisting on perfection in a PTR is a common form of resistance to change and to closure.

12 Work Plan

A work plan outlines the key phases in an initiative and what will be accomplished in each phase, including the main activities in sequence. It is based on a logical flow that stakeholders review and confirm as appropriate to guide the process toward expected outputs and outcomes.

The work plan section includes the following:

- Process overview (listing main planning phases based on a logical flow)
- Title and outline for each phase (specifying starting and completion times)

- Main action items in each phase
- Main deliverables for each phase
- Estimated resources

This is a key part of designing the overall initiative and its phases. It also provides a high-level view of what will happen during specific meetings, sessions, and workshops. The best process work plan represents your PTR in action: it is clear, simple, appropriately sequenced, and attuned to the specific needs of those involved.

SAMPLE QUESTIONS FOR DEVELOPING A WORK PLAN

Are key stakeholders comfortable with the resources required to achieve the purpose and objectives?

Are key stakeholders confident that the resources are or will be in place to support the initiative?

Are the milestones in the plan well situated, appropriately timed, and achievable?

Do the milestones identify specific numbers to support outputs? For example, thirty employees will participate in a minimum of three strategy sessions with resulting reports distributed to all senior managers.

Does the work plan respect the norms for working together outlined in the process assumptions section?

Have the stakeholders each confirmed the logical flow of the work plan from their perspective?

How committed is your client to the implementation phase, or to working with others to implement next steps once the initial process is complete?

How does the work plan support the PTR sections on purpose and objectives, assumptions, and key considerations?

How does the work plan support the implementation of key values at the heart of the process, such as mutual respect and transparency? For example, is enough time provided to respect other commitments in people's lives and to ensure appropriate discussion of issues?

How does your work plan promote accountability for outcomes?

Is the length and intensity of the work plan appropriate for the people who will be involved in each phase?

- Are the outcomes for this initiative deliverable within the phases and time lines of the plan?

- How do you plan to link the results of the process to established operational and strategic plans?

- To what extent can you guarantee each of the outcomes?

- Is it reasonable to hold members of the Steering Committee or other stakeholders responsible for specified outcomes?

- In what ways will the process fulfill or exceed stakeholder expectations?

PRACTICE GUIDELINES: WORK PLAN

- Customize your work plan to the terminology, approaches, and corporate traditions of the clients responsible for following through on the plan. This involves some discussion among stakeholders to ensure that everyone is comfortable with how things will proceed.

- The work plan is developed by the leadership of an initiative (for example, a steering committee or corporate planning group) and is therefore a fairly high-level, strategic document. Management then follows through with an operational plan (often called a project charter) for implementing each phase.

  Process consultants need to be clear about which aspects of a work plan are strategic and which are operational to prevent confusion about roles and responsibilities, while keeping in mind that some overlap between leadership and management perspectives is essential for coordination purposes.

- Monitor milestones and communicate with stakeholders in a frank and supportive manner about progress and pitfalls. Leave the operational details to managers or whoever is responsible for implementation.

- It is common to have some parts of a process already in progress before a work plan is created. Sometimes a client will have a clear picture of an agenda and specific outputs in mind before beginning to develop a plan to achieve those ends. To identify what is already in progress, it's useful to say, "Let's clarify what has been done and what needs to be done on this project. What is already in place? What ideas do you have that are partly formed? What parts of this project have not been initiated at all?"

- Identify concerns that the client may have in relation to planning. For example, "When it comes to planning, what have you learned in the past from processes similar to this one?" or "What are your pet peeves about planning these kinds of processes?"

- Determine what kind of plan the client prefers. A simple plan—usually for a short time frame—is best for a single workshop or meeting that is preceded by preparatory steps and followed by actions to support implementation. It lists main action items and who does what. Simple plans are more common where the relationship between client and consultant is trusting.

  A complex plan is required for multiphase, longer processes involving extensive collaboration among a range of stakeholders; work plans evolve to meet the changing needs of the process. Be prepared for what initially seemed to be a simple plan to morph into a complex process and vice versa.

EXAMPLE: A SIMPLE WORK PLAN

Research Consortium

Planning committee members (already determined) met with the process consultant on [date] to discuss the conclusions reached at their preceding meeting and decide on an appropriate process for analyzing issues and developing recommendations. After considerable discussion, a decision was made to take several steps:

a. Prepare a PTR for review by the planning committee. (Action: process consultant with client) *April*

Research Consortium, Cont'd.

---

b. Develop supportive background materials for review by the planning committee. (Action: head of research consortium with assistance from process consultant) *April*

c. Develop a draft interview protocol for review by the planning committee. (Action: process consultant) *April*

d. Interview planning committee members and others designated by the planning committee and client. (Action: process consultant with input from planning committee on the interview protocol) *May*

> Although this plan looks straightforward and fairly simple, that doesn't mean the process itself was simple—quite the contrary.

e. Prepare a report on interviews and questionnaires and distribute to planning committee members. (Action: process consultant) *May*

f. Review the report and prepare for June planning committee meeting where results will be discussed and recommendations developed for next steps. (Action: client in collaboration with process consultant) *May*

g. Meet with planning committee members to review the report, debrief the process, and decide on next steps. (Action: all) *June*

EXAMPLE: A COMPLEX WORK PLAN

National Process to Identify and Address Issues
Related to the Advancement of a Profession

Phase 1: Initiation of a National Process *(March–June)*

a. Form interim steering committee and initiate the process. The Process Steering Committee (PSC) meets (via teleconferences and in person) to hire an external process consultant and confirm location, resources, and other logistical arrangements and develop a PTR. (Action: executive sponsor)

(continued on next page)

12

National Process to Identify and Address Issues
Related to the Advancement of a Profession, Cont'd.

---

b. Identify background information and consultations fundamental to the success of the process—earlier workshops and reports, policies, who should be consulted, who should advise, and so on. (Action: PSC, which now includes the process consultant)

c. Set criteria for participation and send out invitations for both the consultations and the workshop. (Action: PSC)

Phase 2: Consultations *(August–October)*

d. Conduct opportunistic consultations during or attached to existing meetings of key stakeholders. (Action: process consultant with assistance from PSC on meeting identification)

e. Prepare a report on the results of the consultations for review by the PSC. Finalize the report. (Action: process consultant)

Phase 3: Supportive Information for the Process *(May–October)*

f. Identify required documents and authors and provide a context and framework for discussions during the workshop. Set up work plan for document preparation. (Action: primary client)

g. Review background documents to ensure they drive directly into the workshop process, outputs, and outcomes. (Action: PSC)

h. Prepare a draft policy paper to serve as a central discussion document during the workshop. (Action: primary client commissions paper; PSC reviews)

i. Test the draft policy paper with selected experts and prepare report on feedback. (Action: process consultant)

Phase 4: Pre-workshop Questionnaires *(November–December)*

j. Gather feedback on the policy paper and input to the workshop process through questionnaires with workshop participants. Prepare a report that synthesizes questionnaire responses, providing input to the agenda and a starting point for discussions during the workshop. (Action: process consultant)

**National Process to Identify and Address Issues
Related to the Advancement of a Profession, Cont'd.**

Phase 5: Workshop and Report *(January–February)*

k. Develop and send out pre-workshop packages in first week of January and finalize logistical arrangements. (Action: administrative support)

l. Hold the workshop at the end of February. (Action: all)

m. Debrief the process with the PSC. Write and distribute a report on the workshop. Distribute the report to workshop participants for review. Finalize the workshop report. (Action: process consultant)

n. Initiate the communication strategy developed at the workshop. (Action: PSC)

Phase 6: Evaluation *(one year following the final report)*

o. Initiate an evaluation of the full process, in particular key components and follow-through. (Action: external evaluation consultant)

p. Determine key components of the evaluation. For example, assess progress and momentum in identified challenge areas, measure collaborative research funding established post-workshop, document mechanisms for promoting the profession as identified during the workshop. (Action: process consultant and PSC)

q. Write and distribute a report on the evaluation. (Action: external evaluation consultant)

r. Meet to debrief the process and note key learnings. (Action: PSC)

PROPOSITIONS

50. Most process work plans do not start at the beginning. They start wherever current realities demand that they start.

51. A simple work plan may disguise a complex process.

52. Having a work plan builds confidence among stakeholders that something organized and dependable is going to happen. This may not turn out to be what happens—nor is it necessarily desirable that it do so.

13 Governance

The best process governance structures are simple, efficient, and elegant. They support stakeholders in working together to provide oversight, complete tasks, manage issues, and make decisions.

The intent, size, and shape of a governance structure needs to support the intent, size, and shape of the process plan. A planning group of three or four key people may be all that is required for a one-day corporate planning workshop; an international congress may require a multilayered structure involving an inter-country program committee, session task groups, and a scientific advisory panel, as well as operations and logistics groups.

The governance section of a PTR is made up of the following provisions:

- Leadership function: names, roles, and responsibilities including the executive sponsor, clients, facilitative leadership

- Management function: names, roles, responsibilities

- Structure: committees, groups and their mandates, members and their roles and responsibilities, and how decisions will be made

- Support mechanisms and resources—for example, administrative secretariat, funding, volunteers, sponsorship

- Relevant contracts and accountabilities

> A process is a temporary organization; as such, it requires governance functions to support its work, which are similar to—although much smaller than—those in established organizations.

SAMPLE QUESTIONS FOR DEVELOPING A GOVERNANCE STRUCTURE

What is the smallest and most efficient structure we can use and yet still ensure that we have the necessary functions to support this process?

Does the proposed structure for this initiative

- Accommodate the start-up phase along with other predictable phases of the process such as growth, decline, possible renewal?

- Match the intended process outputs and outcomes in intention and size?

- Include mechanisms for infrastructure and logistical support?

- Sustain effective communication among all those involved (internally and externally) on a regular basis?

- Support managers in following through on decisions?
- Have the architecture to enable comprehensive evaluation during and after the process?

How can we develop a structure that will support effective communication among stakeholders as the project evolves? How can we populate the structure and with whom?

How can we ensure that the results of this initiative are extended into other related areas of interest, both internal and external?

How can we spread representation, expertise, and decision-making power among committees so that each is small and efficient and yet also includes a range of perspectives?

How does the governance structure connect and support interactions among stakeholders?

How is the power (discussed in Chapter Four) required to support this initiative represented and supported in this structure? Is this appropriate?

How will we make decisions: consensus, majority of 51 percent, majority of 75 percent, on the basis of positional authority? (See Chapter Ten.) How can we ensure that our structure supports our approach to decision making?

Is there a need to protect leadership positions in the structure from the possibility of legal action?

What can we do in terms of transparency to ensure that the formal (written) and informal (unwritten, everyday relationships) structures are as similar as possible?

What capacities do we require that we need to find or contract out (for example, report writing, document preparation, logistics)?

What stakeholder capacities does this process require that we already have in place on our planning committee (for example, big-picture strategic thinkers, people with decision-making authority, influential leaders, implementers with credibility, individuals with collaboration skills)?

Who will external contractors report to for initiation and review of their work?

13

PRACTICE GUIDELINES: GOVERNANCE

- First things first: whether you are an internal or external consultant, don't start work without an agreement (contract, memorandum of understanding, or statement of work) regardless of whether you are being paid or are volunteering your services.

    - Specify exactly who will do what by when with whom and why.

    - Pay particular attention to who is responsible for and accountable in relation to the development and implementation of the process design.

    - Distinguish and make links between the work and time required for both design and facilitation.

- After you have completed a draft governance structure, review your PTR to check that your approach will support each section, specifying achievement of the purpose and objectives, support for key considerations and assumptions, and so on.

- Create a structure that will outlast strong personalities and political sensitivities so that the initiative isn't vulnerable to changes in these areas.

- Ensure that the structure has the necessary mechanisms to support oversight of the initiative, including decision making, financial management, issues analysis, and resolution.

- Establish liaison mechanisms to ensure a seamless relationship between stakeholders who are members of committees and their home organizations and groups. For example, prepare a briefing note that summarizes progress of key committees so that stakeholder committee members can provide it to senior leadership in their own organization or group.

- Explain roles, responsibilities, and accountabilities of committee members clearly, for example:

    - Are substitutes allowed to attend committee meetings if the designated individual is unable to attend? If so, should substitutes be named as secondary committee members and kept up to date as the process matures?

13

- Who has the final word on the organization, preparation, design, branding, and distribution of pre-session materials? Keep your involvement in this item strategic, delegating the work to managers responsible for implementation.

- Will the process consultant or facilitator do the final edit of reports or will that be done by the client's internal communications specialist?

- Include an option to withdraw for committee members if they are unable to follow through.

- Keep in mind that in the context of this process, the client and sponsor and the people representing them are not your friends, although they may be your allies in collaborating with you to support positive outcomes for an initiative.

- Outline briefly in writing the mandate of each committee and expectations of its members. Even if this outline is only a couple of paragraphs, it formalizes and makes transparent the responsibility of membership and the rationale behind it.

- Pay attention to the names of committees and positions in your structure, ensuring that the names reflect accountabilities. People tend to become cynical if committee names are inflated or deflated in comparison to the work being done.

- Wherever possible, set up committees and groups that are inclusive yet still relatively small, so that it is easier to arrange meetings and make decisions. Ask yourself, "Is this the smallest inclusive committee we can have to do this work?"

13

According to a Chinese proverb attributed to Confucius, "The beginning of wisdom is to call things by their right names." Because of the transitory and contingency nature of work relationships, people might have many close associates but few true friends in their professional lives. Thus, unless you are absolutely certain that a colleague is a *friend*, assume that the person is, at best, an ally whose loyalty could quickly evaporate depending on the situation.

—Stybel and Peabody, 2005, pp. 15–16

> The trouble with organizing a thing is that pretty soon folks get to paying more attention to the organization than to what they're organized for.
>
> —Wilder, 1953, p. 214

EXAMPLES: GOVERNANCE STRUCTURES

Training and Development in Facilitation: Regional Public Service Group

---

The organization of this workshop will be led by Learning Solutions Group Managers Jane Smith and John Doe.

Presenters and training materials will be approved by the Regional Centre for Leadership (RCFL) as the governance body for public service corporate learning.

Advisory Group

The role of the Advisory Group is to provide input and feedback, and to support the co-leads. The Advisory Group will consist of the following:

- Chair, Regional Council
- Representatives of Local Councils as identified by their chairs
- Representative, Regional Consultations Project Office
- Representative, Postsecondary Review Secretariat
- Representative, Public Service Organizational Development and Human Resources Networks
- Representative, Region-wide Renewal Initiative

The Advisory Group will meet regularly with the process consultant to prepare a PTR for this initiative and then to discuss and agree on the agenda, format, speakers, and awards.

Support

Administrative support will be through the Regional Human Resources Training Office.

13

European Alliance for Organ and Tissue Donation and Transplantation: National Issues Forum

Steering Committee

The Steering Committee provides input on policy and processes to the initiative. Members provide leadership advice and direction on the Forum, fostering consensus building and promoting change in their respective communities after the Forum. Steering Committee discussions and conclusions are based on consensus.

Responsibilities of the Steering Committee are to

- Review and provide advice on the Forum overview, assumptions, and process
- Contribute to a list of invitees
- Contribute to the meeting process (agenda, speakers, background papers, and so on)
- Meet following the Forum to determine action on the conclusions and recommendations developed at this workshop

Planning Committee

The Forum Planning Committee provides oversight to the initiative. Decisions at Planning Committee meetings are made by consensus.

Responsibilities of the Forum Planning Committee:

- Oversee the preparation of draft documents for review and input by Steering Committee members, including purpose, outcomes, assumptions, background documents, and overall process for the Forum.
- Contribute to the list of participants, limiting guests to seventy (one hundred maximum).
- Plan, prepare, implement, and disseminate results of the Forum.
- Supervise contractors.
- Provide input to background documents such as the pre-Forum questionnaire.
- Collaborate with the facilitator on the meeting process, for example, by suggesting others who can act as table facilitators.

13

(continued on next page)

European Alliance for Organ and Tissue
Donation and Transplantation: National Issues Forum, Cont'd.

The Forum Planning Committee provides strategic advice and decision making on the development of the workshop. Planning Committee members meet by teleconference and in person as required to provide input. Members: [LIST NAMES]

Expert Advisory Committee

Members of the Expert Advisory Committee provide scientific and medical advice to the Forum Planning and Steering Committees. Members are the presidents of professional medical associations responsible for implementing Forum recommendations in the field.

Process Support

The consulting company (ST) is responsible for the meeting design and facilitation, workshop report, and draft request for proposals. It will also provide input and expertise on the overall process as required and in the synthesis of background documents.

ST is responsible for process consulting. Roles of ST company members are as follows:

- *Jane Jones:* client liaison, workshop design, and facilitation, including support to the Planning Committee
- *John James:* background documents, development of pre-workshop interviews, and reporting on interviews
- *Jennifer Junes:* note taking during the workshop, preparation of reports on Summit, and debriefing meeting in collaboration with [name] and the client
- *Jordan Johns:* liaison and administrative support on an as-required basis

The client for this project is the Vice President of the Professional Alliance Group, represented by David Danes.

Governance structures can also be specified in a graphic format, as in the chart that makes up the following example (Figure 13.1).

13

Example: NEW LIGHT Project Industry Development Workshop: Wales

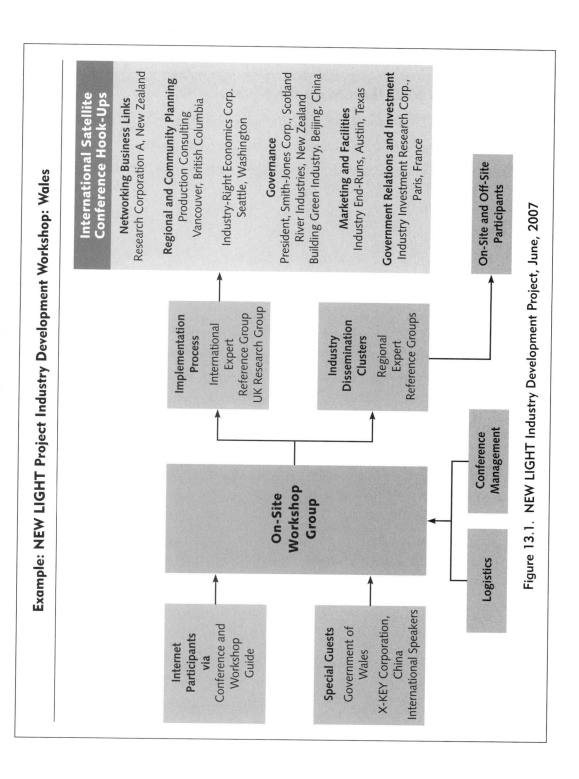

Figure 13.1. NEW LIGHT Industry Development Project, June, 2007

PROPOSITIONS

53. Governance structures must echo the values inherent in the process.

54. Effective governance structures do not yield to petty politics.

55. The most efficient process structures serve both means and ends.

13

14   Essential Documents

The essential documents required to support a process depend on its scope, purpose, objectives, outputs, and outcomes. Some initiatives require extensive information, including comprehensive literature reviews, scientific and legal evidence, surveys, and interviews for decision-making purposes. Other initiatives may be focused more on stakeholders' and participants' bringing their experience, expertise, and opinions to the table. In most settings that involve a range of perspectives at the table, a common glossary and list of key acronyms are essential to support meaningful discussion.

This section in a PTR includes the following items:

Customize! Ensure that supportive information clearly and unambiguously supports the process and is easy to access. The most powerful documents are presented in a way that enables discussion and action in relation to process outcomes.

- Glossary

- Acronyms

- Fact sheets such as prevailing demographics

- Mission, vision, and value statements from key stakeholder organizations

- Stakeholder coordinates

- Existing documents containing information pertinent to the process

- Key background documents to be developed or commissioned

- Additional sources where stakeholders and participants in the process can get more information about various aspects of the initiative

- Reports on the process

Regardless of the size or focus of a process, it helps to approach requirements for essential documents systematically so that participants have what they need in terms of concepts, vocabulary, specific language such as acronyms, content, the organization of complex information, history of the initiative, and tools for decision making.

In addition to gathering information from various established sources, consider how you can tap the minds of those participating in a way that will enable their expertise and points of view to be used concretely in sessions. This may involve pre-session approaches such as telephone interviews, questionnaires, and focus groups, or facilitated discussions during sessions as well as post-session reviews.

Discussions about background documents often surface important considerations and assumptions in a process. For example, coming to agreement on and defining a term such as "knowledge transfer" when some stakeholders prefer to use terms such as "research into practice," "knowledge translation," or "dissemination" enables consensus building.

14

SAMPLE QUESTIONS FOR IDENTIFYING AND DEVELOPING ESSENTIAL DOCUMENTS

Acronyms: What short forms (such as those that represent words and phrases, organizations, technologies, locations, departments) do we all need to be aware of to talk to one another coherently and efficiently?

Existing documents:

- What current materials would help us avoid duplication, scope creep or drift, or infringement on other stakeholder areas?

- What information would help inform us about current concerns and provide credible data to support our initiative?

Fact sheets:

- What facts do all participants need at their fingertips to ensure that discussions are based on common understandings?

- What information would help participants feel more comfortable and confident in this process? (Example: a point-form history of the years preceding the initiative.)

Glossary:

- What words are important to this process and what is our common understanding of what they mean?

- What technical jargon may be known to some participants and unknown to others?

- What terms are people likely to use in different ways depending on their experience? (Examples: *profit, customer service, advocacy, lobbying, client, consultation, advisory.*)

Sensitive words: What words have the potential to be lightning rods for misunderstandings? (Examples: *divestiture, culture, disadvantaged.*)

> Supportive documents are interpreted by process participants based on their perspectives and expected outcomes. Ask questions that stimulate individual and group perspectives on the information provided.

14

Logistics:

- Which documents should we provide on paper and which electronically? By what dates?

- Who will own the copyright for the background documents prepared for this process? Individual writers, the Planning Committee, sponsoring organization, or some combination?

- Will the background documents be refined after the process is finished based on insights gained during the process?

New documents:

- What materials would support the purpose and objectives of this process that we don't already have?

- Which of these materials do we *need to have?*

- Which of these materials would be *nice to have?*

References: Where can we direct stakeholders and participants to get additional information that is easily accessible?

Stakeholder strategies: Whose strategic decisions do we need to be aware of when developing and implementing this process?

PRACTICE GUIDELINES: ESSENTIAL DOCUMENTS

- Avoid duplication. Review each objective and related outcomes to identify what information is required to support discussion and decision making. Look first for existing references that make additional work unnecessary, then decide on background documents that need to be developed to support identified outcomes.

- Clarify up front who will provide various documents. The client is usually the most efficient source of stakeholder coordinates, history, key words, and acronyms.

- Code documents for easy identification throughout the process, for example, distinctive numbering and color.

14

- Ensure that working documents look like drafts rather than final versions so that reviewers feel comfortable marking them up and returning them. For example, for printed documents: use less expensive paper, include a "draft" watermark, and avoid costly color text where possible.

- Give some thought to whether and when documents for a process should be labeled as "draft." Distributing a draft and providing an opportunity for input serves the following purposes:

  - Builds ownership among participants for the views expressed in the paper. If people know that they can influence a discussion paper, they are likely to have more ownership for the process and the paper as a whole when it's completed.

  - Protects the process from becoming overfocused on a document and its author. If the document says it's a draft and someone wants to criticize it or its author on either a factual or opinion basis, then the facilitator can simply say "thank you for the feedback" and add that these views will be considered by the review committee for the next draft.

  - Gives the paper the added credibility of having a group of people from different perspectives discuss it and provide commentary. This tends to make the paper more usable for a broader range of stakeholders after the process is complete.

- Investigate and accommodate (where possible) accepted writing style standards for your client groups.

- Name documents based on what they contribute to a process (say, "Comprehensive Literature Review") rather than on who wrote them ("the Jones paper"), and then use that name consistently in conversation and written materials.

  Options for authorship on documents:

  - Prepared by Ann Annison, Ph.D., in collaboration with the ABCD project steering committee: Bill Billings, Carol Collings, and Dierdre Dawlings, MBA

14

- Prepared by the ABCD project steering committee in collaboration with EFGH consulting group
  - Prepared by Phil Philly, Ph.D., XYZ Survey Group
- Review how information is presented in support of learning and discussion. Does it appeal to a range of learning styles as well as to management and leadership preferences?
- Think about sending participants an electronic version of documents and having them bring their own copies to meetings and workshops.
- Think strategically about the number and type of documents for a session, adjusting the workload to reflect the capacity of a short meeting, extensive consultation, national forum, or local workshop.
  - Consider whether the people involved generally welcome background information or tend to put it aside.
  - Ask yourself what the absolute minimum number of documents is that people require in order to feel comfortable with what they know when working with others. As a general rule, less is more, and less is usually read more than more.
- When commissioning the development of a document, you can save a lot of time and energy by providing the contractor with a detailed outline of requirements for submitting papers to your group. (See the "Quality Checklist" presented later in this chapter.)
- Where longer, more complex documents are required, include a short, point-form cover sheet to provide an overview that focuses specifically on key discussion points related to the purpose and objectives of the process. This cover sheet is in addition to an executive summary: its purpose is to highlight key items related to a specific initiative.

Interpreting Materials from Multiple Sources

Processes often require the development of a background piece based on information from multiple sources that must be gathered, interpreted, and synthesized into a single document for easy access by participants.

14

Here are four steps to gathering and interpreting information from multiple sources.

Step One: Gather and bring information related to an initiative together in one location such as an electronic database. Information may include official documents and position statements, recorded interviews or written notes, reports on questionnaires and surveys, key background information, guidelines, standards, policies, and legislation.

> Our beliefs about things are constructed; they result from a synthesis. The issue is whether the construction will be reliable and responsible or indulgent, slapdash and delusory.
> —Taylor, 1995, p. 102

Step Two: Edit and reorganize the information for clarity and accessibility, and to preserve the confidentiality of those involved. Maintain links to original sources while removing original context. For example, parts of a document may be selected on the basis of their relationship to an initiative's objectives; responses to a specific interview question may be included with responses to other questions. This reorganizing of original materials creates a new "whole" related to a specific initiative.

Step Three: Synthesize the original information into key categories and themes. This requires moving away from original surface realities and adding meaning within the context of the PTR and the writer's knowledge of the situation. For process consultants, this is often the point where the interpretation process ends. Further interpretation needs to involve stakeholders and other participants in the design. At this point the document is distributed to some or all participants in the process for review and as a *starting point* for discussion.

This reorganization of materials is reflected in the introduction to the background document. For example:

> Preparing this report involved transposing questionnaire and interview responses electronically, removing personal references to individuals while retaining central points, and interpreting and grouping key points, question by question, into similar categories based on their contents. Wherever possible, respondents' original words and phrases are used to represent what a number of responses indicated.

14

Step Four: Have process participants review the background document and interpret it based on their experience and understanding of the situation. The document is now subsumed within the design process. In this approach, reliability is usually not an issue as each process is unique.

Validity is determined by process participants. If the document is a report that summarizes their perspectives (gained through interviews or questionnaires) you ask whether the report accurately represents their views. If the document is intended to be a background paper to kick-start discussion and decision making, then you ask whether they are comfortable moving forward with this document for that purpose.

> The mind fits the world and shapes it as a river fits and shapes its own banks.
> —Dillard, 1982, p. 15

Whether you're working with a report or a background paper, be clear about next steps. If the document is a report on interviews or question-naires, let participants know that it will be used to kick-start discussions and then will be out of date: it is final in its current format. If the document is a summary of existing research, you may want to invite those engaged in the process to provide feedback on the paper and contribute to its final version. This expands ownership for the document in the field and enhances its credibility.

Reports

Reports on processes serve several functions:

- Enable verification of what has happened in a process by confirming the content with key participants.

- Provide a record of actions for monitoring process outcomes and implementation.

- Identify factors affecting the implementation of outcomes.

- Build ownership for next steps during or after a process.

- Enable check-in for increased accountability.

- Support leadership for implementation.

14

- Include a list of who participated in the process in support of further connections and joint actions throughout other phases of an initiative.

Clarifying the purpose of a post-process report and how it will be developed and finalized can prevent disruptive misunderstandings down the road. Here are some guidelines to support a preventive approach:

- *Consider how the report will be used and what you can do to support that use.* How can it be formatted and presented in a way that will be appealing to various groups?

- *Customize each report on a process in the same way that you customize a design.* Consider an innovative approach such as a video developed by group members so that you can communicate the flavor of the process as well as the content.

- *Build in mechanisms to support transparency in report writing.* For example, designate the process steering committee or the external (and objective) process consultant as having final approval. You can also make it clear at the outset of the process that key stakeholders will review and confirm that the report reflects their understandings of the process conclusions.

- *Avoid overproducing working reports by providing colorful, expensively designed paper copies.* You are more likely to betray environmental concerns than impress stakeholders.

Quality Checklist for Working Documents

A working document is a document *in progress* that will be enhanced by the insights of individuals involved in a process. Working documents are converted to their final form at the conclusion of a process.

Working documents provide a basis for planning, designing, and implementing processes. They are driven by what is practical—what works for a process—and by their consequences in terms of the information people need and want with respect to the scope, purpose, and objectives of an initiative.

By providing writers with clear expectations about what you want, you can save a lot of time and frustration that would otherwise be spent in unnecessary

14

redrafting. Customize the quality checklist presented in this section (available for download at www.strachan-tomlinson.com) for working documents to suit your specific situation.

Working documents are often composites of information produced for other purposes, such as published research, literature reviews, policy statements, previously commissioned reports, trend analyses, meeting reports, or official statements. It is rare that these existing documents can be applied directly. They need to be interpreted and modified, and this involves accurate reading, rational analysis and synthesis, rewriting, and reformatting to ensure that the final product is relevant, accurate, clear, and appropriately formatted, and then reviewed and edited.

Use or customize the following checklist as a detailed guide for writers contracted to produce materials for a process.

Quality Checklist

Relevance: Are contents pertinent to the scope, purpose, and objectives outlined in the PTR and the overall situation?

- [ ] Is the underlying perspective in line with the process overview, that is, scope, purpose, objectives, outputs, outcomes?
- [ ] Is the information directly applicable to the task at hand?
- [ ] Is all relevant information present?
- [ ] Are parts of the document more useful than others? If yes, describe.
- [ ] Does the document fulfill contractual obligations?

Accuracy and Integrity: Are the contents faithful to original sources?

- [ ] Are all sources clearly identified and referenced with Internet links provided where appropriate and available?
- [ ] Are conclusions based on reliable evidence?
- [ ] Are comparisons based on data from compatible sources?
- [ ] Are materials even-handed (that is, not biased toward a particular view of the issues), and are all positions identified and clearly represented?
- [ ] Are authors' personal views presented separately from a disinterested representation of the information?

14

☐ Are statistical summaries and comparisons based on an understanding of how statistical data are developed and interpreted?

☐ Are summaries of concepts and ideas a true reflection of original materials?

Writing Clarity: Can the intended audience read, understand, and (if appropriate) begin to act upon the document the first time it is read?

☐ Are scientific or jargon terms appropriate to the intended readers?

☐ Are sentences short and to the point?

☐ Does the language reflect and enable clear thinking?

☐ Have the authors avoided common metaphors and clichés?

☐ Is information presented using the minimum number of words, sentences, and paragraphs?

☐ Is the language active, crisp, and professional?

Presentation: Is the document formatted to enable participants to read, understand, and apply the information? Does the document

☐ Have a covering page with a name or title, whom it is for, when it was written and by whom, and number of the draft?

☐ Include a table of contents with corresponding page numbers?

☐ Provide an introduction that sets out why the document was developed (its rationale and assumptions), how it is intended to be used, by whom and under what circumstances, methodology (rationale and approach to information gathering), data sources, and so on?

☐ Have clearly identifiable sections and levels of headings?

☐ Conform to the style sheet template requirements provided by the contractor, with consistent visual and electronic formatting throughout?

☐ Contain simple illustrations, charts, and graphs where appropriate?

☐ Display printed text in a pleasing and artful manner?

Review: Has the document been reviewed and edited by a committee of experts and a professional editor for

☐ Relevance and accuracy?

☐ Language and presentation?

14

EXAMPLES: ESSENTIAL DOCUMENTS

Glossary: Planning Committee Meeting—
Council on the Environment

Consensus: Substantial agreement—the degree of consensus that has been achieved is measured through one of the following positions:

- I agree with the proposal
- I can live with the proposal
- I disagree, or remain undecided

Silence is not interpreted as consent.

Outlook: Describes the Council's preferred future; involves revising 2005–2006 and extending to 2006–2007; provides a realistic stretch for the organization; motivates Council members and others.

Stakeholders: Those who have a vested interest in the success of the Council: volunteer organizations working in "healthy environments," environmental scientists and their professional associations, advocacy groups, senior government personnel.

Strategic Priorities: These are based on pressing issues or challenges affecting the achievement of the Council mandate, initiatives, and deliverables. They fit within the Council's Strategic Framework for sustainability of National Parks; describe a major area of responsibility and commitment for the Council; are based on stakeholder needs and expectations; require collaboration among stakeholders to be successful; and result in a realistic stretch for the Council.

14

The next example is a commentary to support a steering committee's decision about the meaning of the term *advisory* for a national, eighteen-month public sector consensus-building forum. This commentary resulted from comprehensive deliberations by a national, multidisciplinary, and cross-sectoral steering committee. After this document was prepared and approved for this initiative, the term *advisory* as defined therein was included in the Core Assumptions section (Chapter Ten) of the PTR for this client.

Defining a Contentious Key Word

What does "advisory" mean in national health strategy processes?

(Process Consultants' Commentary)

Governments and other policymakers are clear that the role of advisory committees is to enable individuals with appropriate education, experience, and expertise to consider identified issues and provide the results of their deliberations to policymakers in the form of recommendations; that is, they advise. The governments' and policymakers' roles are then to pass those recommendations on to appropriate action areas.

Health professionals are impatient with lengthy processes for the development of recommendations and with the increasing time lag between recommendations and action. As a result, the nature of their participation on advisory committees has evolved to include action and advocacy in addition to advice.

History: In the 1980s and 1990s, many health professionals agreed to provide the benefit of their experience and expertise as advisers on committees related to a wide range of initiatives sponsored by government and nongovernment organizations. Their role was to provide advice in the form of recommendations that would proceed to higher levels for further discussion, revision, and approval.

Over the past several years, volunteer health professionals have expressed increasing dissatisfaction with their advisory roles for a variety of reasons:

- They did not see enough or any concrete action as a result of their efforts.

- Committee processes frequently took longer than they perceived necessary.

- Frequent changes in political and bureaucratic leadership meant that many processes changed or stopped in midstream, with recommendations being shelved.

This experience prompted a new approach by volunteer health professionals toward participation on advisory committees. They made clear their greater expectation of return on their investments, for example, through opportunities to act with fellow health professionals and other concerned stakeholders in the area under consideration by building on the results of the advisory process in their professional communities.

14

(continued on next page)

Defining a Contentious Key Word, Cont'd.

Implications for this Council and its Committees:

a. Health professionals on advisory committees perceive themselves to be in partnership with governments, nongovernment organizations, and policy-makers rather than in service to them as advisers. This results in a *give-get* relationship with respect to facilitated processes, with health professionals *giving* advice and *getting* an opportunity for collaborative approaches to health system change.

    Professional societies and associations recognize that they can usually act faster and with fewer encumbrances than government. In an effort to decrease the time lag between recommendations and action, many of these organizations have redefined their roles in advisory processes to emphasize their stake as partners in early dissemination, implementation, and knowledge translation strategies.

b. Professional societies are educating their members about fiduciary respon-sibilities with respect to the health of patients. Members at advisory tables now sit with more experience and training about how to advocate on behalf of their societies and patients in discussions with governments, nongovern-ment organizations, pharmaceutical suppliers, and other stakeholders. This advocacy experience frequently translates into another give-get strategy; that is, their advice comes in exchange for an opportunity to advocate on key society-specific issues, for example, on the rights of patients to the best quality treatment possible.

c. Time is a scarce commodity for health professionals, who are experiencing increasing demands on their schedules in addition to their personal com-mitments and professional responsibilities. A frequently heard comment is, "Can you guarantee me that this event will have a significant impact on professional practice after this process is concluded?"

d. Societies of health professionals are increasingly allying themselves with nongovernment organizations and other stakeholders (in research, for example), who share their values and commitments in terms of patient health. These alliances generally serve the advocacy interests of their member organizations.

    The ultimate result is that increasing pressure is brought to bear on advisory committees to ensure that their work does not end only in

14

Defining a Contentious Key Word, Cont'd.

recommendations but in action that will further the aims of these alliances. Participants are often selected to take part in a process because they can wear more than one hat—bring more than one perspective to bear—during discussions. Others consult with sister organizations to ensure that they are up to date on recent positions with respect to key recommendations.

In conclusion, the term *advisory* is evolving in response to policy changes in the health field, many of which (innovative partnerships, for example) are supported by governments. Invitees to advisory committee processes are becoming increasingly assertive about the need for constructive and efficient partner-based approaches in which they want to have an opportunity both to *give* advice and to *get* a venue in which they can initiate changes that will ultimately benefit patient health.

From our perspective as process consultants, this dual approach is a positive one, as it enables all parties to develop approaches that are more focused, productive, and outcomes-oriented. It also ensures that volunteer committee members feel satisfied as a result of their involvement—a key prerequisite to successful implementation and eventual system change.

Paul Tomlinson, Ed.D., and Dorothy Strachan
Process Consultants, ABC Planning Committee

14

PROPOSITIONS

56. Key words with unconfirmed meanings breed values tensions.

57. The purpose of a document within a process is the basis for determining the best technology to communicate its contents.

58. When it comes to background information, less is usually more, and less is usually read more than more.

15 PTR—Three Examples

$\mathbf{A}$s the examples in this chapter demonstrate, each PTR is customized to the process and the people involved: each has a different look and also varies in terms of approach, headings, language, and the amount of detail provided. The bottom line is whether the PTR serves the interests of those involved in developing, managing, designing, and facilitating the initiative.

The first example is for regional account planning in a multinational high-technology corporation that already has a standardized approach to planning, including financial sales goals on a Web site dashboard. This PTR was developed on the basis of discussions with the client and a needs assessment with account managers. We then implemented account planning sessions with six accounts in a division. To produce the document shown in this example, account managers in a regional sales group met to design and implement a standardized account planning process for their region. The emphasis was on a "sound-bite" approach in the PTR and relatively little up-front planning. The result is a relatively concise, simple PTR.

The second example describes a process through which three faith-based nonprofit boards in a region could speak with one strong and clear voice to a nongovernment regional authority charged with service oversight, monitoring, and surveillance.

The third example is for the first phase of a complex, multiphased, multiple-year national health initiative on organ donation and transplantation that was being implemented in collaboration with key stakeholders in local, regional, national, and international settings. This PTR (reprinted with permission of the Canadian Council for Donation and Transplantation) is the basis for the case study in Part Four, which is focused on developing evidence-based questions for a national forum on kidney allocation.

Account Planning for a Regional Sales Group

Situation
Last year:

- New team; building experience with the account; finding our way as a team.
- We established a baseline for how we work together.
- We were successful in many ways.
- We also learned over the year how we want to change for this year so that we can focus a little more on process and use those changes to help us meet plan for the upcoming year.
- We developed an excellent plan last year and we followed it simply because at some level some of us had internalized the plan and the whole team worked together to stay on track; we didn't have an active monitoring process, but we still accomplished our goals—a significant achievement.

This year:

- We are a team with a year under our belts; we have considerable experience with the account.
- We are clearly on track financially.
- We need to acknowledge our successes over the past year and build on those for the coming year so that we can maintain our momentum.
- Our theme is "Building New Bridges to PQR"; that is, we have some sales bridges in place and we need to build on those achievements and add some more.

Purpose
Our general purpose is to do strategic planning for the PQR account, traditionally one of our biggest earners. The outcomes we want are a plan for achieving revenue goals and a plan for enhancing how team members work together on a day-to-day basis.

15

Account Planning for a Regional Sales Group, Cont'd.

Stakeholders

From one perspective, all current and future customers are potential stakeholders. However, for the specific purposes of this planning process, we have two stakeholders: our client who buys products and services from us, and our sales personnel.

Core Assumptions

- We need to review our high-level goals and priorities and either confirm or adjust them slightly, and then, when we are on the same wavelength, to look at tactical action plans.
- Our sales targets for the next two quarters are to meet or exceed 15 percent over earnings on the past twelve months.
- Our two biggest competitors have targeted PQR over the next two years and their service delivery is better than ours. We can't count on past performance or established relationships to hand us orders over the fax machine. We are going to need to have a greater on-site relationship at PQR.
- We need to clarify and consolidate our marketing messages.
- Everyone on the team is expected to take action items during this process. Senior management are engaged in a support capacity.
- As a team we need to continue to mature so that we all take ownership for the plan; we need to function more interdependently so that all our actions are more closely linked to the updated PQR vision.
- This process is also about maturing as a sales team: to be successful we need to enjoy working together to meet common goals; this means ownership and buy-in for all of us in relation to both revenue goals and interpersonal relationships.
- We need to develop another quality plan with the following changes from last year:
  - Use our existing plan as a baseline (don't reinvent the wheel).
  - Use the summary of pre-workshop questionnaires and discussions to inform how we select opportunities as well as to identify issues that affect how we work together and address them.

15

(continued on next page)

Account Planning for a Regional Sales Group, Cont'd.

- Develop a regular monitoring system that involves the core group in revisiting the plan regularly to assess progress.
- Listen actively to what PQR wants later this morning and use their expectations to guide revisions to the existing plan.

Key Considerations

- We have significant challenges on our plate: new markets are exploding; new management at PQR makes it much like calling on a new account; new relationships are required to develop within a changing business model in which there is movement more to solutions and problem solving.
- PQR corporation is experiencing a real downturn. They have been an important client in the past but may figure as a smaller profit center for us in the future. How can we support them to continue to be successful?
- We achieved three out of six prioritized opportunities with PQR based on last year's plan. On the upside we have some really strong relationships with individual buyers who like our products and want to continue expanding our base with them. On the downside our main block was our inability to provide on-time, on-target technology support services to the same extent as our competitors. Because PQR is big enough to have several suppliers, its people are in an ideal position to compare support services and therefore make performance-based sales decisions in the future. In summary, our products are stellar and our service needs improvement.
- We have intelligence about our executive-level partner relationships and the extent to which we are being outsold by our biggest competitor.

Essential Documents

- Report on interviews with team members and senior executives in our company.
- Presentations by PQR executives at our workshop. They will outline their feedback on our performance over the past twelve months and their expectations for the next twelve months, including their new IT planning architecture and business development goals.

15

Account Planning for a Regional Sales Group, Cont'd.

- Illustrations to map the bridges metaphor.
- Summary of customer service statistics.

Process Plan

This year's theme is "Building New Bridges"—both to our customers and among ourselves as we get ready for another successful year of working together.

Phase I: Get the information we need to plan successfully. Do a needs assessment with sales personnel and interview senior executives regarding expectations for the sales team.

Phase II: Convene a workshop where we can develop a realistic plan that also pushes our organization.

Phase III: Prepare a report on the workshop. Prepare a briefing note for senior PQR executives to let them know how we are following up on their presentations and our strategic priorities.

Workshop Agenda Flow

Part I: Getting Rolling

Part II: PQR Expectations

Part III: Building the Plan

Part IV: Team Development: Issues into Answers

Part V: Planning into Action: Who Does What by When

Planning Structure

A small planning committee including the regional manager, head of marketing, and a representative from the sales force will work with the process consultant to make this workshop happen. The process consultant is responsible for initiating and managing the process.

15

Three Boards Speaking with One Voice

Context

This process engages three boards of directors and their related organizations' senior staff in ABC Community Corporation (a health group) in a process to learn about one another and begin to work collaboratively in support of a mutual vision of excellence.

- ABC Main Board has oversight accountability for seven institutions, four residences, and three long-term care facilities.
- ABC Research Institute conducts research specific to the priorities of the Main Board.
- ABC Foundation raises funds to support both the ABC Main Board and the Research Institute.

Each board is distinct and represents the oversight for its associated entity. At the same time, each board is interdependent with the others. The lead board is ABC Main Board.

Although the three boards and the organizations they represent have experienced significant success over the past few years, they have never met together and generally know very little about each other.

The decision by state government three years ago to initiate regional oversight authorities (ROA) within the state has made obvious the need for a process where board members can learn about each other and look for ways to provide coordinated leadership in this new reality of the ROA, particularly given that four strategic priorities of the ROA are directly related to our strategic priorities.

In terms of governance, ABC Main Board has one board member on the Foundation Board and three members on the Research Institute Board. The ABC Foundation Board chair is a member of the ABC Main Board.

- The Research Institute Board is experiencing funding challenges and wants direction from the Main Board on priorities. The Foundation Board is trying to determine fundraising priorities and needs direction from both the Main Board and Research Institute Board.
- The Main Board and the organizations under its purview have been in a state of transition since the new CEO came in three years ago. She has a different management style from her predecessor's; that is, the

15

Three Boards Speaking with One Voice, Cont'd.

previous leader was more directive and less hands-on. The current leader is more engaged and collaborative.

- The mission and vision of the main board changed in 2004 and are not clear, nor are they used to anchor strategic planning.
- The Research Institute had its annual planning day recently, and the purpose was to discuss a recent five-year review. The planning report outlines six key recommendations, the most important being a need for the institute to focus on identified priorities rather than responding to financial opportunities as they arise.

Focus

Purpose: The ABC Main Board is convening a retreat with the ABC Research Institute Board and the ABC Foundation Board to develop a clearer understanding of how all three boards can support a shared vision focused on excellence.

The objectives of this retreat are

a. To provide an opportunity for members of the three boards to learn about each board's mission, values and guiding principles, vision, strategic priorities, key partnerships, budget overview

b. To update board members briefly on the ROA initiative and discuss how the three boards can support each other in this emerging context

c. For each board to

- Identify strategic challenges that would benefit from support by the other boards
- Define what "excellence" is for each identified strategic challenge

d. To develop recommended actions for how the boards can support one another in addressing these strategic challenges and strive to achieve a common vision focused on excellence

Retreat Outputs (shorter term)

- Background document comparing key elements of the three organizations

15

(continued on next page)

Three Boards Speaking with One Voice, Cont'd.

- Background document providing an update on the ROA
- A report on the retreat outlining key discussion points and conclusions
- Recommended action steps for each board to take on identified strategic challenges

Retreat Outcomes (longer term)

- Enhanced common understanding among the three boards about what they do and how they can support one another
- Enhanced and more frequent communication among the three boards regarding mutual support in strategic challenge areas
- A process to identify important emerging issues and how they can be addressed in the future

Stakeholders

In a broad sense, every individual who benefits from using our superior service, facilities, and faith-based philosophy has a stake in how well we do with respect to this planning process. Stakeholders at this retreat will include board members and senior management from all three boards and their related organizations.

Assumptions

- The retreat provides an opportunity for participants to learn about each other's boards, to discuss identified issues and explore where there is agreement on what to do next. It is not a decision-making venue. The report on the retreat will go back to each board for consideration and development of next steps.
- There is a need for all three boards to think in a more strategic and integrated manner.
- Although there is some concern about whether the vision statement is appropriate, it will not be reviewed at this retreat.
- The mission statement is currently under review by the Mission Effectiveness Committee and will be accepted as is for the purposes of this retreat.

15

Three Boards Speaking with One Voice, Cont'd.

- The ABC Foundation is engaged in a branding initiative designed to identify and address challenges related to the three boards working together. This retreat will not address branding.

- This retreat focuses on two issues of common concern that have been identified by a joint Chairs and CEOs committee. This is not a comprehensive strategic planning session.

Key Considerations

- Each of the three organizations is successful as a separate entity. However, they are not mutually supportive and they could contribute significantly to each other's increased success.

- Lack of clarity about how the three boards relate to one another is a source of tension.

- Since the ROA was announced by the state three years ago, our perspective has evolved from viewing it as a threat to seeing it as an opportunity. The ROA is still trying to figure out how it will function and its people need our leadership and experience to be effective. Our elected representatives have made it clear that the ROA is to function within a collaborative local approach and we can provide significant leadership in our domain.

- Consultants for branding have been selected, and this will have implications for all three entities; for example, possible name change, key messages that will be piloted six months after the retreat.

- Board evaluations are in progress and will be distributed four or five months after the retreat. We will need to review the evaluation report in the context of the retreat report.

Essential Documents

a. Key terms and acronyms

b. Glossary of key terms including *partner, partnerships, determinants, strategic*

(continued on next page)

15

Three Boards Speaking with One Voice, Cont'd.

---

c. A comparative document on the three organizations with the following headings:

- Date of establishment
- Mission
- Vision
- Values
- Strategic priorities
- Contributions and expectations of each other
- Future strategic challenges
- Key partners
- Budget: revenues and expenses, net
- Financial contributions to each area
- Key e-documents to prepare for this meeting

d. Visual schematic of the three boards working together

e. Overview of the state environmental network plan

f. Membership and positions for each board

g. Map to retreat location

Process Plan

The process consultants for this initiative will commence and drive the work plan.

Phase I: Prepare and review background information
Design and facilitate initial Retreat Planning Committee meeting to be held the week of February 5.

In collaboration with client, prepare a PTR for the retreat, including purpose, objectives, outputs, outcomes, context, key considerations, assumptions, identification of essential documents, structure.

Phase II: Observe meetings related to the retreat as designated by the client, such as branding committee
Facilitate a meeting with the three board chairs and three CEOs to determine strategic issues to address at the retreat.

Prepare and confirm a brief report on the meeting.

Prepare retreat agenda, design, worksheets, report outline.

15

Three Boards Speaking with One Voice, Cont'd.

Phase III: Facilitate the retreat in May

Work with an independent report writer to finalize the report and confirm it with participants.

Structure

Our new Joint Governance Committee for the three boards is the planning committee for this session.

A group composed of board chairs and organization CEOs will convene to review the PTR and decide on three or four strategic challenges for the retreat to address.

The primary client for this process is the director of strategic planning and the Joint Governance Committee. Administrative support will be supplied by the Office of the Director of Strategic Planning.

15

Access to Organ Transplantation in Canada: Phase 1—Kidney Allocation

A Working Document by Steering Committee Members Not for Distribution

Overview

The Canadian Council for Donation and Transplantation (CCDT) was established in October 2001 to improve organ and tissue donation and transplantation in Canada. The CCDT is an independent, not-for-profit corporation mandated to provide advice to the federal and provincial territorial Conference of Deputy Ministers of Health (CDM) in support of its efforts to coordinate federal, provincial and territorial activities relating to organ donation and transplantation.

The CCDT has three standing committees: Donation, Organ Transplantation, and Tissue Banking and Transplantation, as well as working groups that include non-Council experts. The standing committees bring forward standards, policies, and best practices for ratification by Council. An ethicist supports the three committees in their identification and analysis of ethical issues.

The CCDT Organ Transplantation Committee (OTC) is developing a framework for action at local, provincial or territorial, and national levels that will result in a sustained, systematic approach to organ allocation. This framework will be based on evidence provided through a review of existing practices, policies, or guidelines (national and international), a review of science and literature, and expert consensus.

The OTC initiatives relate to components of transplantation such as (a) optimally supporting and referring potential transplant recipients, (b) assessing and listing patients waiting for transplants, (c) exploring opportunities and challenges of living donation, (d) optimally monitoring and evaluating transplant recipients, and (e) optimizing organ utilization and allocation.

To date, the CCDT has hosted four Forum processes designed to consult with health professionals and other stakeholders on best practices that can inform recommendations to the Conference of Deputy Ministers of Health:

> *Severe Brain Injury to Neurological Determination of Death* (April 2003) focused on development of a national agreement on the processes of care, commencing with severe brain injury and culminating with neurological determination of death.

15

Access to Organ Transplantation in Canada: Phase 1—Kidney Allocation, Cont'd.

Medical Management to Maximize Donor Organ Potential (February 2004) developed guidelines and standards that will enable Canadian health professionals to maximize donor organ potential.

Assessment and Management of Immunologic Risk in Transplantation (January 2005) developed consensus recommendations to improve immunologic risk assessment and management in transplantation.

Donation After Cardiocirculatory Determination of Death (February 2005) produced guidelines to inform health care systems that are developing programs for donation after cardiocirculatory death.

The Access to Organ Transplantation in Canada initiative will recommend the components of a model for allocating organs (kidney, heart, liver, and lung) to patients on waitlists. Allocation models for each organ type will be developed separately and common issues will be identified.

Heart, liver, and lung allocation models will be developed in collaboration with the Canadian Society of Transplantation organ-specific working groups and perhaps through other CCDT organ-specific initiatives such as the one for kidneys. The final CCDT report will contain recommendations for allocation models for all transplantable organs.

Understanding Kidney Allocation

The process from identification of renal disease in a patient to transplantation of a deceased donor organ involves many steps:

1. Referral from family physician or pediatrician to a nephrologist.

2. Discussion of transplantation between primary nephrologist and patient.

3. Referral to transplant program.

4. Completion of transplant evaluation, which may include consultation with other specialists.

5. Decision about eligibility for transplantation, made by transplant team.

6. If patient is eligible for transplant, review option of living kidney donation.

15

(continued on next page)

Access to Organ Transplantation in Canada:
Phase 1—Kidney Allocation, Cont'd.

---

7. If no potential living donor, activate patient on donor waitlist.

8. Allocate kidneys to waitlist candidates.

9. Transplant surgery and post-transplant management of patient by transplant program.

The Kidney Allocation Initiative will focus entirely on step 8—allocation of the deceased donor kidneys to patients on the waitlist.

Purpose, Objectives, and Scope

The aim is to develop a step-by-step decision-making model that is acceptable, useful, and adaptable within unique regions across the country. This initiative will provide an opportunity for discussion and agreement on the key components of a deceased donor kidney allocation model. Objectives are

1. Identify factors (medical, legal, ethical, logistical, and administrative) that contribute to transparent and equitable kidney allocation practice.

2. Develop a kidney allocation model that incorporates the factors in objective 1 and is flexible enough to adapt to regional applications.

3. Enhance transparency and improve public confidence in the Canadian transplantation system.

4. Identify important areas of research for kidney allocation.

The scope of the kidney allocation initiative is to address how deceased and nondirected living donor kidneys are allocated to adult and pediatric patients on waitlists. The model will include kidney and kidney/pancreas allocation only.

The model will not include

- Allocation of organs from directed living donors.
- Allocation of deceased donor islet cells.
- Allocation of list exchange kidneys.
- Paired or living donor exchange models; this is being addressed within another initiative.
- Tissue allocation; this is being addressed within the tissue banking initiative.

Access to Organ Transplantation in Canada:
Phase 1—Kidney Allocation, Cont'd.

Outcomes

Immediate outcomes

Provide recommendations for the transplant community on allocation of deceased donor kidneys.

Provide advice on the recommended components and practices for improved kidney allocation in Canada to the Conference of Deputy Ministers of Health.

Intermediate and long-term outcomes

The deceased donor kidney allocation initiative will result in

Consistent and transparent kidney allocation in Canada.

Recommendations for a kidney allocation model to contribute to the development of government policy and appropriate funding for allocation of kidneys and transplant patient care in Canada.

Enhanced confidence in the Canadian transplantation system by members of the public and health care professionals.

Increased health services research opportunities in kidney allocation.

Recommendations to address gaps in infrastructure support.

Outputs

Outputs are the deliverables that will be produced in the project in order to achieve the desired outcomes. They include

1. Literature reviews and synthesis of the data and evidence on the following topics:

   1.1 HLA matching

   1.2 Waiting time (including preemptive transplantation)

   1.3 Impact of adult and pediatric donor and recipient age (including age matching)

15

(continued on next page)

Access to Organ Transplantation in Canada: Phase 1—Kidney Allocation, Cont'd.

1.4 Ethical and legal issues related to kidney allocation (including an assessment of waiting time)

1.5 Expanded criteria for donors and dual kidney transplants

1.6 Allocation of kidneys when considering a kidney/pancreas transplant

1.7 Urgent medical conditions

1.8 Diabetes and other diseases re: access to organs

1.9 Organ sharing—benefits and drawbacks (international, provincial experiences).

2. Survey and report on current practices on how kidneys are allocated.

3. Scan of existing models of renal organ allocation in Canada and internationally. For example, the United Network for Organ Sharing in the USA, Eurotransplant, United Kingdom Transplant, Australia and New Zealand Dialysis and Transplant Registry.

- Description of the algorithm (for example, HLA, waiting time).
- What systems are used to track and report?
- How is compliance measured?
- Can they project changes in their model (modeling database)?
- Is there a "best" model, and if so, how can we "canadianize" it?
- Average waiting times for different blood groups—pediatric versus adult.
- Average waiting times for combined kidney/pancreas versus kidney alone.

4. Identification of the perspectives of the informed public and renal patients (Kidney Foundation) regarding kidney allocation. Possibly an "educated" public consultation (regional focus groups and report).

5. Host a National Forum of approximately 125 participants to

- Discuss and recommend best practice for Canada.
- Derive a consensus for a transparent model for kidney allocation in Canada.

15

Access to Organ Transplantation in Canada:
Phase 1—Kidney Allocation, Cont'd.

---

6. Produce a final report that will include the following:
- Overview of process to develop organ allocation models
- Glossary
- Ethical and legal considerations
- Overview of existing models around the world
- Summary of the evidence
- Recommendations for kidney allocation model
- Implementation considerations
- Knowledge transfer
- Participants

7. Incorporate Kidney Allocation Initiative report into Access to Organ Transplantation document with other organ-specific reports.

Assumptions

Core assumptions are the agreed-upon givens that provide a common starting point for reflection, discussion, and decision making. They outline the perspective within which a process unfolds and help ensure that everyone involved is on the same page, that is, focused on a common purpose and objectives.

The key assumptions underlying this initiative are as follows:

1. Optimal organ allocation is the process by which kidneys are allocated in an equitable (not equal) and transparent way to patients who are waiting for transplantation.

2. Patient need for deceased donor organs outstrips supply, and as a result decisions must be made about which patient among the many waiting will receive a kidney for transplantation.

3. The gap between supply of and demand for organs makes equity and transparency in the allocation process essential.

4. Allocation of a scarce resource (such as transplantable organs) must be done fairly, considering both equitable access and optimal outcomes for transplantation.

15

(continued on next page)

Access to Organ Transplantation in Canada:
Phase 1—Kidney Allocation, Cont'd.

5. Developing an organ allocation model does not dictate medical practice, but it provides a framework for operations. Individual physicians will continue to make decisions regarding individual patients.

6. The model will focus on allocation of deceased and nondirected living donor organs.

7. The kidney allocation initiative will incorporate organ sharing for sensitized patients as previously recommended ("Assessment and Management of Immunologic Risk in Transplantation: A CCDT Consensus Forum" 2005) but will not otherwise include organ sharing across jurisdictions.

8. Policies and approaches that are specific to the Canadian health care system are necessary for accountability.

Participants

Participants include representatives and perspectives from major stakeholder groups including transplant programs, governments, organ donor organizations, bioethics experts, the public, legal experts, and others as determined by the Steering Committee.

Key Considerations

The following important circumstances, facts, data, and concerns will be taken into account due to their potential impact on the success of the kidney allocation initiative:

1. There is regional variability in Canada with regard to waiting times for deceased donor kidney transplants. Differences in current organ allocation practices in part reflect differences in deceased donor rates within regions of Canada.

2. Consensus guidelines on eligibility criteria for kidney transplantation have been developed by the Canadian Society of Transplantation (CST) Kidney Working Group and have been accepted for publication by the *Canadian Medical Association Journal*.

3. The applicability of kidney allocation models used by other countries will inform the project.

15

Access to Organ Transplantation in Canada: Phase 1—Kidney Allocation, Cont'd.

---

4. Increased incidence of end-stage renal disease will escalate the need for donor organs. Paradigms for kidney allocation will need to evolve as need escalates.

5. Prolonged exposure to dialysis while on the waitlist for transplantation is associated with increased mortality.

6. Transplantation is more beneficial for children and adolescents (because of the potential for growth, education, quality of life); consequently, prioritization of children should be considered.

7. Acceptance and implementation of a kidney allocation model will require thoughtful implementation strategies, recognizing the unique needs of regions, programs, and health care professionals.

8. CCDT is sponsoring two related projects in 2005 and 2006, including a report to consider the feasibility of a national paired donor exchange registry and an information management initiative.

Structure

CCDT Council: The CCDT comprises fifteen members plus a chair and includes representatives of key professional donation and transplantation organizations, nongovernment organizations, the ethics community, the spiritual and pastoral care community, and transplant recipients and donor families. The Council oversees the development and endorses advice for the Conference of Deputy Ministers.

CCDT Organ Transplantation Committee: The role of the CCDT Organ Transplantation Committee is to commence the initiative, provide a basic steering framework, endorse the funding, and enable implementation through the provision of appropriate resources and support. The chair of the OT committee is the official link between the CCDT Board of Directors and the Access to Organ Transplantation initiative. The OT Committee is responsible for reviewing the recommendations to the Conference of Deputy Ministers of Health based on the initiative outcomes.

15

(continued on next page)

Access to Organ Transplantation in Canada:
Phase 1—Kidney Allocation, Cont'd.

Initiative Steering Committee: The Initiative Steering Committee provides input on policies and processes for initiative activities. Members provide leadership advice and direction on the activities, fostering consensus building and promoting change in their respective communities after completion of initiative activities. Steering Committee discussions and conclusions are based on consensus.

Responsibilities of Steering Committee members are to

- Review and provide advice on the purpose, outputs, outcomes, assumptions, key considerations, and overall process of the initiative.
- Provide expert advice as required on background documents, speakers, expert committees.
- Contribute to a list of invitees to meetings, consultations, or forums.
- Contribute to the meeting process, for example, the agenda, introductory speakers, background papers.
- Where appropriate, support implementation of the initiative recommendations.

The Steering Committee will participate in one face-to-face meeting and two teleconferences. Travel and accommodation expenses are covered by the CCDT as per current policy.

Planning Committee: The Planning Committee is the core working group providing oversight for the initiative. It is led by its chair, with the CCDT lead being the current CEO. Strachan-Tomlinson will provide support as process consultants. This includes both design and facilitation of the initiative throughout its various phases.

Forum Recommendations Group: If a forum is chosen as the best process for developing the model, a Forum Recommendations Group (FRG) will meet prior to and during the Forum to consider draft recommendations and develop a final report. The FRG will consist of Steering Committee members and other identified experts whose contributions will enhance the quality and credibility of the initiative process and final report. An FRG member will be present at each table during group discussions and will represent that table's conclusions during later deliberations.

15

Access to Organ Transplantation in Canada: Phase 1—Kidney Allocation, Cont'd.

FRG members include

- Medical society representatives who bring their individual expertise and the perspectives of their societies to the FRG table but do not formally represent their societies in terms of decision making.
- Individuals with content expertise and experience and a commitment to implementation in the field after the Forum.

(CCDT lead and process consultants will support the FRG.)

FRG Membership: [Names deleted for privacy.]

Evaluation, Communication, and Knowledge Transfer

This aspect of the initiative will be developed and implemented by CCDT senior management in accord with current policies.

15

PART 4

EXPERTS AND EVIDENCE IN CONCERT

Over the past several years, we have seen an increasing need to bring together subject matter experts to explore the best evidence available and come to agreement on complex—often interdisciplinary and multisectoral—issues in a specific field. Whereas most process designs have a primary focus on one or two areas such as team development, issues analysis, or planning, these designs usually have a multiple focus on several areas, and involve collaborative decision making about technical or scientific inquiries affecting a field.

The decisions made in these processes usually affect a large number of stakeholders and are based on the highest-quality evidence and expertise to support knowledge transfer and the implementation of conclusions in a field. The final products are referred to in a variety of ways; they may be guidelines, standards, data elements, policies, rules, or legislation.

Because the prime drivers in these processes are evidence- and expertise-based questions, a central challenge is to build agreement among those with a stake in the issue regarding what needs to be asked. Responding to this challenge requires considerable thought, and as a result it typically takes more time to develop these questions than to answer them. That is, it may take a committee working together over a few months to come up with a comprehensive and sound list of questions, which can then be answered in a three-day workshop or a series of consecutive task force meetings.

In summary, in these process designs, the questions asked are as important as the answers. Part Four outlines a process for developing these questions.

Chapter Sixteen describes the need for and the rationale underlying process designs that support an expert- and evidence-based approach to building agreement.

Chapter Seventeen outlines a process for developing questions. This process follows through on the PTR for "Access to Organ Transplantation in Canada—Phase I Kidney Allocation" described in Chapter Fifteen. In this case, following the development of agreement on relevant questions, a national forum was held with fifty-six expert participants who developed a national consensus on responses to expertise- and evidence-based questions in a three-day workshop (Knoll and others, 2007).

16 Why Evidence-Based Solutions Now?

One unique feature of a design requiring an evidence-based solution is the need for a substantial investment in evidence-based questions. For example, say that health professionals in a country near yours have a broad range of approaches for how they diagnose and treat malaria. Epidemiological data show that some regions of the country have significantly fewer deaths and health complications related to malaria than other regions.

You have been contacted by the minister of health for this country. She commissioned a peer-reviewed study six months ago that concluded that the differences among regions reflected variations in health policy and medical practice.

She wants to act on this study and so is looking for an objective, external process consultant who can work with a national multidisciplinary group of experts to design and facilitate a process to develop national guidelines for the diagnosis and treatment of malaria. The minister emphasized that this process must be based on the best science available, and must enable implementation of these new guidelines across quite different regions of the country and across a broad range of health professionals.

KNOWING WHAT TO ASK

In situations like this one, a key element in the process is knowing what questions to ask to get the answers required to develop the guidelines. Therefore an essential step in the process design is to bring together content experts with the client and other stakeholders and the best evidence available in a collaborative, consensus-based process for question development. This process begins as soon as a PTR is in place.

Answers to evidence-based, question-driven processes like this one are usually responses to content-specific, technical policy development challenges. They may include a broad range of requirements such as data elements for a security surveillance system, industry-wide guidelines on liability insurance for micro businesses, legislation and policies for equitable access to legal counsel for low-income individuals, clinical practice guidelines for health professionals, policies for ecosystem management of wild animal disease, or safety standards for a cross-jurisdictional regulatory body.

In situations like these—where both potential questions and their answers involve cross-sector, multiperspective problems—a collaborative, consensus-based approach engages individuals, groups, and organizations with a stake in both developing the questions and implementing the answers. This approach also helps ensure that the eventual recommendations and decisions required to enable change are seeded in the evidence behind how the questions are framed.

What is unique about processes for creating questions collaboratively?

First, a lot is at stake in the answers to the questions. Because these answers will guide the behavior of individuals, groups, organizations, and jurisdictions in the field, stakeholders have a significant investment in outputs and outcomes. The questions must direct discussion and decision-making efforts toward knowledge transfer and implementation of decisions.

Second, the best evidence available is required to help shape the questions. Knowing what to ask involves extensive background documentation, such as reviewing the scientific literature related to the issue, tracking down what is currently done in the field with respect to the issue, documenting legal and ethical implications of the questions, exploring expert experience, finding out how others address this issue in their jurisdictions, and conducting surveys to explore what stakeholders think regarding what needs to be done. In the end, the questions are asked of the evidence as well as of experts and other stakeholders.

> The bottom line is that the more focused, specific, and evidence-based the questions, the higher the likelihood that the resulting decisions or recommendations will be implemented in the field.

16

Third, the process for developing agreement on the questions is rigorous and comprehensive. It requires an inclusive, comprehensive approach involving key influencers and representatives of organizational authorities to build ownership for implementation of the answers.

WHY BEST EVIDENCE IS IMPORTANT

Best evidence is an essential tool for technical and scientific decision making. *Evidence-based* means that both the questions and their answers are based on the highest-quality facts and information available, from all perspectives, in relation to a problem. This approach enables individuals with various perspectives on an issue to have confidence in both the questions and the answers.

Various sectors and jurisdictions take different approaches to using evidence as a basis for action. Evidence-based government has become a major part of many governments' approaches to policymaking and to the machinery of government. The driving force for evidence in government tends to be the type of question being asked, rather than any particular research method or design. Types of evidence—all of which are focused on impact—include ethical, implementation, descriptive, analytical, attitudinal, statistical modeling, and economic (Davies, 2004, adapted).

Evidence-based medicine is "the integration of best research evidence with clinical expertise and patient values." In medicine, the quality of evidence is graded according to specifically defined levels such as systematic reviews, randomized controlled trials, observational studies, opinion and experiences (OpenClinical, 2007). In the environmental area, evidence-based reasoning focuses on decision making related to the interactions among people, technologies, and ecosystems. The primary value espoused is respect for scientific evidence in collaborative decision-making processes involving knowledgeable stakeholders.

These are the core assumptions underlying an evidence-based approach:

- Stakeholders from a range of perspectives have identified a problem whose resolution requires comprehensive background information.

- Collaborative, inclusive, consensus-based decision making by experts will produce the best questions and answers.

16

225

- Both the questions and answers will be developed by knowledgeable individuals who will bring their experience and expertise to the table to review and interpret the best evidence available. These individuals will have a range of perspectives and views regarding what questions need to be asked, how they should be formulated, and what the correct answers might be.

- What can be included as evidence and the levels of strength of evidence are specific to the problem area and will influence decision making in the field.

- Those responding to the questions and implementing the answers need to be aware of the evidence and the strength it has to support or influence their decisions and actions.

Judgment based on experience and expertise may be of critical significance in those situations where the existing evidence is equivocal, imperfect or non-existent.

—Grimshaw and others, 2003

Be transparent about the strength of evidence: include a reference to it in the background documentation for each question. Many urgent problems require solutions for which the evidence to support decision making is relatively weak. Nonetheless, it is important to make a recommendation based on the best evidence available combined with expert opinion.

AMBIGUITY, PARADOX, AND DISAGREEMENT

Three challenges support the need for evidenced-based process design: ambiguity, paradox, and disagreement. Most situations that require a process consultant have some degree of uncertainty and confusion. To complicate this ambiguity, these situations are also often fraught with paradox: what seems self-evident to some participants is counterintuitive to others; what are perceived to be facts by some are branded as fiction by others. The third challenge involves the enormous quantities of information that are available today and the fact that reasonable, competent experts will disagree on the meaning of that information in relation to issues being discussed.

16

Through an evidenced-based design, process consultants face these three challenges head-on. They enable knowledgeable stakeholders to develop and address targeted questions using the best available information to come to agreement on decisions that can be acted on in a specific area.

PROPOSITIONS

59. Creating evidence-based process designs requires patience and persistence in the face of impatience and acquiescence.

60. Bringing experts and evidence together boils down to doing the best you can with the best you can get.

61. The most savage controversies are those about matters as to which there is no good evidence either way. (Bertrand Russell)

16

17 A Design for Developing Evidence-Based Questions

In this design, questions are developed collaboratively through a rigorous, facilitated, consensus-building process that takes questions through several drafts before completion, as outlined in the following six steps:

1. Create a Questions Development Group (QDG).

2. Get suggestions for questions from a range of stakeholders.

3. Develop a questions flowchart including categories and related questions.

4. Circulate the questions flowchart for feedback.

5. Find or develop the background information.

6. Finalize the flowchart and related background information.

WORKING THROUGH THE STEPS

Although these six steps are presented as a sequence, they may happen in various ways, depending on the expertise of those involved. For example, the first two steps may happen in twenty minutes during a meeting of key stakeholders. Or a literature review may have been done recently by another organization or a commissioned contractor and therefore only require an update, resulting in steps 1, 2, and 5 happening in the first hour of a committee meeting.

17

1. Create a questions development group.

In evidence-based decision-making processes the evidence does not speak for itself. People bring their experience to the evidence to develop the questions as well as to answer them.

Members of the Questions Development Group (QDG) must be able to maintain and support their unique perspectives while collaborating with others to produce the best possible questions to drive change in their field. The following steps will promote the development of a satisfactory QDG:

a. Find a leader with strong personal and professional credibility in the field who is willing to chair the QDG and be accountable for high-quality, timely question development. Select the leader carefully, ensuring that you have someone who is willing to lend personal credibility both to the questions development process and to the implementation of the answers. Sometimes the chair of the QDG is also the chair of the process planning committee.

b. Engage three or four credible experts with different perspectives to work with the chair and be responsible for question development.

c. Review Chapters Two and Three of this book to determine which perspectives and powers you need on this committee to support its work.

At the initial meeting of the QDG, confirm that group members will make decisions and work together using an inclusive, consensus-based decision-making approach to support later implementation of answers.

> Include someone in your QDG who has a propensity for questioning the conventional wisdom in that field.

2. Get suggestions from a range of stakeholders.

People who have been consulted on questions for a process build ownership for the responses to those questions, whether or not their specific questions are included in the final design.

Much depends on how you ask for input from stakeholders. Be transparent and straightforward when you make this request, whether you are brainstorming the questions in a face-to-face meeting (for example, among planning committee members), exploring options on a teleconference, or asking for input in writing.

230

Include the purpose, objectives, and scope in the request for questions. Explain that not all questions will be included in the final process design. Name the members of the QDG and support the group's credibility by providing a two-sentence bio for each person and describing very briefly the process to be used for developing the final questions.

3. Develop a questions flowchart.

Developing evidence-based questions that will result in evidence-based answers means that a number of decisions must be made ahead of time. These decisions can happen in many different ways. The approach that follows represents the order used in recent questions development processes and reflects the perspective of the facilitator in a face-to-face meeting of the QDG.

- Review and confirm the challenge embedded in the problem under discussion by completing the sentence, "The challenge in this problem is to—"
- Ask QDG members to jot down what they think are the top five or six big questions that this process must address.
- Review with the QDG the list of brainstormed questions generated during other meetings, such as with a planning committee.
- Bring together group members' prioritized lists and those brainstormed by planning committee members. Note areas of agreement. Discuss remaining areas. Create a draft list of main categories or problem areas and group the questions into the categories.
- Develop a questions flowchart that provides a logical framework for how the categories and questions will be ordered for discussion and decision making in the process design. Pay attention to key turning points (decision points) in the process to make these decisions.

Ensure that the questions flowchart conforms with and supports the way implementation of decisions will happen in the field. These flowcharts may take several approaches—for example, chronological, thematic, decision tree, or based on urgency or harm reduction.

- Check the final flow, categories, and related questions with a larger committee in your structure, such as a steering committee.
- Integrate their feedback into a final questions flowchart.

Here is a sample questions flowchart for the national kidney allocation guidelines process presented as the last example of a PTR in Chapter Fifteen. This flowchart has three main categories and a total of seventeen main questions. Note the technical and scientific nature of these evidence-based questions.

Questions Flowchart:
National Kidney Allocation Guidelines

Part A: HLA Matching and Sensitization

A1. Should HLA matching be included in a Canadian Algorithm? If yes, check all that apply: (a) zero mismatch (ABDR), (b) 1A and B and zero DR mismatch, (c) DR matching, (d) B matching, (e) A matching. Note related key considerations. If no, why not?

A2. Canadian stakeholders have confirmed that one or two kidneys would be preferentially allocated to highly sensitized patients with PRA $\geq$ 80%. Should sensitization be included in the local and regional allocation of kidneys? If yes, to what degree: (a) $\geq$ 20%, (b) $\geq$ 50%, (c) $\geq$ 80%? Note related key considerations. If no, why not?

Part B: Wait Time

B1. Should wait time be included in a Canadian Algorithm? If yes, suggest key considerations. If no, why not?

B2. Should patients be allowed to accrue wait time prior to dialysis? If yes, beginning at what level of kidney function: (a) GFR $\leq$ 20, (b) GFR $\leq$ 15, (c) GFR $\leq$ 10? If yes, suggest key considerations. If no, why not?

B3. When should wait time start for patients on dialysis? Check the best option: (a) date ready for listing (evaluation completed), (b) dialysis start date. Note key considerations.

17

Questions Flowchart:
National Kidney Allocation Guidelines, Cont'd.

B4. Should the start of wait time for re-transplant be different from that for first transplant? If yes, how should it differ? If no, why not?

B5. Should patients with early graft failure (that is, < 90 days), retain previously accrued wait time? If yes, key considerations? If no, why not?

B6. Should patients not yet on dialysis be allowed to receive a deceased or nondirected living donor kidney transplant? If yes, why? If no, why not?

Part C: Medical Issues

C1. Should children (18 and under) receive priority consideration in a Canadian allocation scheme? If yes, why? If no, why not?

C2. In adults (19 and over), should younger recipient age be given priority in a Canadian allocation scheme? If yes, should you assign weighting for (a) each specific age, (b) age categories (e.g. 30–40 years), (c) other: . . . ? Note key considerations. If no, why not?

C3. Should donor and recipient age matching be used in a Canadian allocation scheme? If yes, should you (a) match old to old (as in the Euro-Transplant Seniors Program), (b) match young to young, (c) minimize the difference between donor and recipient age (as with U.K. Transplant), (d) other: . . . Note key considerations. If no, why not?

C4. Do you agree with the current U.S. definition of ECD (expanded criteria donor)? If yes, why? If no, why not?

C5. Should ECD kidneys be allocated by the same algorithm as standard criteria donors? If yes, why? If no, how would you allocate differently?

C6. Should there be a separate list for patients waiting for ECD kidneys? If yes, why? If no, why not?

If yes, should patients be allowed to be on both ECD and regular lists? If yes, why? If no, what not?

C7. Should patients waiting for a combined kidney-pancreas transplant receive priority consideration over patients waiting for a solitary kidney transplant? If yes, how would you give priority? If no, why not?

(continued on next page)

Questions Flowchart:
National Kidney Allocation Guidelines, Cont'd.

C8. Should other combined transplants (for example, liver-kidney) be considered in the Canadian Algorithm? If yes, why? If no, why not?

C9. Should medical urgency be considered in the Canadian Algorithm? If yes, check all that apply: (a) unable to dialyze (PD or hemo) due to access issues, (b) severe uremic neuropathy, (c) severe uremic cardiomyopathy, (d) other: (specify). Indicate key considerations that apply. If no, why not?

If medical urgency is to be considered, which of the following decision-making processes should be used? Check all that apply: (a) consensus among Tx program members, (b) periodic review of clinical status, (c) documentation that other therapy has been optimized, including dialysis, (d) other: (specify). Indicate key considerations that apply. If no, why not?

Source: Knoll and others, 2007, pp. 13-14.

Once you have a draft questions flowchart in place:

- Identify the groups that will be affected by responses to the questions. If representatives of those groups are not on your planning committee or QDG, check the questions with group members to ensure that they fit the practical realities of the situation. At the same time, ask about the best evidence required to support discussion and decision making.

- Agree on which questions this initiative could explore but will not address, so as to limit discussion to what can be reasonably accomplished in the process. This clarification sets boundaries based on the objectives for the initiative and supports discussions about scope in the PTR (discussed in Chapter Ten).

4. Circulate the questions flowchart for feedback.

Solicit input from the parent committee for the QDG, asking their members to review the flowchart and provide feedback. Sample questions:

- Do the questions address your understanding of the objectives, scope, and proposed outcomes for the initiative?

- Does the order in which questions are asked in the flowchart reflect your experience with this issue?

- To what extent could answers to these questions have a significant positive impact on what happens in the field with respect to key issues?

- Do individual questions need changes, additions, deletions? Please comment.

Keep in mind that in evidence-based question development, *robust* means sturdy and strongly made, based on a vigorous process and reviewed by peers.

5. Develop background information.

Track down or commission the strongest possible evidence to support key stakeholders in answering the questions in each part of the flowchart. The following steps will help ensure thorough background development:

a. Conduct a literature review to find out what is known and not known in the research with respect to questions in the flowchart.

b. Commission surveys and papers for areas where evidence is lacking.

c. Ask recognized and authoritative leaders in the field to consult with colleagues and develop expert opinion pieces for issues in the flowchart where credible evidence is lacking.

d. Find conclusions and recommendations that have been created through processes in other jurisdictions where the focus was on similar or related issues—for example, at international meetings, in legal decisions, through advocacy for policy development.

e. Where required, commission legal and ethical perspectives on key issues to support informed decision making.

f. Determine whether the process used to develop the questions and related evidence meet the test for excellence in the problem area.

Find a quality checklist or tool specific to the area in which the questions are being developed.

In health care the AGREE instrument (Appraisal of Guidelines for Research and Evaluation) helps groups creating questions for the development of clinical practice guidelines to do an overall assessment of guideline quality. This instrument also defines key health-related terms for use in guideline development processes and provides suggestions for knowledge translation into the health care field, for example, in relation to the strength of recommendations resulting from questions. Country-specific cases are also included. For more information, see the Agree Collaboration Web site, www.agreecollaboration.org.

6. Finalize the flowchart and related background information.

Review the questions one last time with QDG members, using the background information to support discussion.

a. Consult the literature review regarding the veracity of the questions: Are the question areas correct? Which questions seem most pertinent? Least pertinent? Are any questions missing? What assumptions (if any) are contained in these questions? Is there evidence for these assumptions?

b. Based on the questions flowchart, evidence in the literature review, commissioned surveys, and papers and feedback from the parent committee, refine the questions with QDG members and distribute any remaining concerns about questions to get specific expert input for a final review. For example, you may want to have a conversation about terminology with someone who is a respected expert in that area.

c. Convene a meeting of the QDG to develop a final version of the questions:

(1) Integrate feedback from the expert stakeholder group.

(2) Estimate the time required to answer each question based on the process involved. For example, "Assuming that we have excellent evidence to support discussion, what is your best guess for how long it would take a table of eight experts with different perspectives to answer this question in a consensus-building workshop?"

(3) Identify the evidence required to support stakeholders in discussing and coming to agreement on answers to questions.

(4) Review the order in which questions will be asked within the flowchart, making conscious decisions about what should be asked first and last. Use the time estimates to shape the process design.

(5) Prepare final questions as handouts for discussion. Make it easy for people to review the evidence when discussing a question by attaching excerpts from relevant evidence to each handout and providing time during a process to review this information prior to discussing its implications. This approach assists respondents in bringing their experience together with the best evidence available to develop insightful recommendations. Encourage participants to detach the evidence when discussing questions so that they have both in front of them at the same time.

PRACTICE GUIDELINES: QUESTION DEVELOPMENT

Developing evidence-based questions for technical and scientific solutions is an enticing design challenge for process consultants. In these situations it is common to have lack of clarity about who is a stakeholder, disparity of power and resources among stakeholders, potentially competing interests among clients—contact, primary, intermediate, and ultimate (described in Chapter Two)—that must be addressed collaboratively, complex problems that are not well defined, scientific uncertainty, inadequate background information, differing perspectives that have caused or have the potential to lead to adversarial relationships, as well as dissatisfaction with previous and existing approaches and processes.

Given these realities, it is important to have several conditions in place to support a collaborative approach (Gray, 1989, pp. 5–15, adapted; Winer, 1994, pp. 21–25, adapted):

- Stakeholders are interdependent.
- Stakeholders have access to the best evidence available and are willing to contribute it or find it.
- Stakeholders have a vested interest in making change in the field.
- Solutions emerge by understanding commonalities and dealing constructively with differences.
- Decisions about final questions and the evidence for decision making are jointly owned.
- Stakeholders assume collective responsibility for acting on responses to questions.

17

Build a strong and authoritative core questions group.

The expertise and authority of the QDG chair and committee members is essential to the development of credible questions and answers.

The answers to evidence-based questions end up being guidelines for "what works" and how things should be done differently in a problem area. As a result, it is important to build ownership for implementing "what works" by engaging organizational representatives of those who will apply and eventually implement the recommendations in the problem area. Be clear with committee members that they are lending their good names to the entire process, including the questions and the resulting answers, and also committing themselves to support implementation in the field.

In many processes, those who develop the questions are a smaller subgroup of a steering committee and their work is reviewed by a parent steering committee. Review the list of potential stakeholders in Chapter Nine when considering who might be potential contributors to developing evidence-based questions. Not every one of the groups listed in Chapter Nine needs to be involved; some will only need to be consulted; others may be helpful in reviewing drafts; others may simply not be appropriate.

Include the perspectives of marginalized groups when developing these questions. These groups often have reasons to mistrust mainstream data and research and may also have different perspectives on what constitutes a strong level of evidence than others involved in the collaboration. Consider issues related to race, ethnicity, culture, sexual orientation, class, and gender to avoid exacerbating concerns related to bias based on power imbalances, lack of trust, and insensitive interviewing or data collection. Research is often described as scientific—but it can also be political, racist, or classist (Annie E. Casey Foundation, 2002, adapted).

Authoritative and credible leaders and committee members are usually busy people and often serve as volunteers in evidence-based decision-making processes.

> The greater the credibility and engagement of experts in the development of questions and how they should flow, the greater the likelihood of timely implementation of answers in the field. Define the term *expert* with care: the meaning is usually situation- and sector-dependent.

238

Provide the administrative support to enable them to be successful when working with others—for example, by setting up meetings, putting technology support in place, and finding resources for surveys and research.

Some leaders in a field may have a strong commitment to the issues being discussed but may not have the time to be on a committee. Consider setting up an ad hoc group of experts who can make available limited amounts of time for discussions about specific questions and for reviewing documents.

Clarify incentives for stakeholder engagement in developing questions.

Stakeholders are more likely to become involved in developing evidence-based questions when they are clear about the potential benefits (Gray, 1989, p. 34). Look for beneficial connections like these:

- Could increased public awareness about global warming drive the development of *new policies* to support environmental health?

- Will questions about biological therapies result in *better outcomes for patients* who are being treated according to outdated medical protocols?

- Is technological change providing the possibility of *more efficient and less expensive* garbage pickup in your city?

- Will the process support the development of *intersectoral partnerships* as an important opportunity for shared problem solving and decision-making among stakeholders?

- Could responses to questions support the development of an *international research collaborative* based on shared data and information analysis?

Name and define what action the answers to your questions will require.

What will the answers be called: guidelines, professional standards, legal standards, legislation, goals, rules, practice parameters, field policies, recommendations, regulations?

Naming the type of answers you are seeking can support implementation strategies: the term *guidelines* has a specific meaning that varies from sector to sector,

17

as do terms such as *recommendations, standards, rules, regulations, laws, legislation, practice parameters,* or *field policies.* Be clear about the level of authority for implementation that the answers will have: strict enforcement, encouragement to comply, leadership influence, incentives for compliance, used in conjunction with professional judgment, monitored by professional society for compliance, supported by public sector endorsement.

Your evidence-based questions could result in new garbage pickup protocols for your city that are monitored as part of the city's quality control project for urban renewal. A result for a different process might be the development of Clinical Practice Guidelines for how physicians treat skin cancer. Another result might be goals in an international accord such as the Kyoto agreement that encourages compliance through public ratification. Or perhaps the product might be revised national standards for airport wildlife control that will be monitored and enforced through international air traffic regulations.

Address intellectual property questions.

Before you start to develop the answers, address intellectual property issues related to the conclusions. What will the report be called? Who will be the primary and secondary authors? Will the final document be copyrighted by the sponsoring organizations? Do you need to have contributing committee members and report writers sign a copyright agreement before agreeing to sit on a committee?

Conduct a cost-benefit analysis of a collaborative approach.

Consider the time, energy, and financial resources required to develop and respond to questions using a collaborative approach. Will the cost of this approach result in benefits that merit the resources expended? To whom should this information be communicated?

In many situations where evidence-based questions may be required, the potential benefits far outweigh the costs. For example, the resources required for preparation and research on evidence-based questions would clearly be justified for the development of effective clean water policies to protect the environment or standards for expanding liability insurance coverage to micro-size businesses.

Enable both face-to-face and virtual communication when developing questions.

There are various benefits to having electronic, telephone, and face-to-face communication among those developing evidence-based questions. Consider the following factors when deciding how to communicate:

- How are people in this area comfortable communicating?

- What logistics will affect scheduling meetings? For example, consider the needs of senior leaders who may travel a lot, engineers who work in a variety of locations, professors and teachers who have scheduled classes, physicians who must be on call, homemakers who need to find child care, and so on.

- How much ownership do committee members have for implementing the answers to the questions? Face-to-face discussions are often useful when working through complex challenges involving territorial issues.

- What technical tools do you have available to facilitate discussion and decision making? For example, you may be able to provide space on a protected Web site, conference calls, or a company wiki.

> Decide on *how* to communicate after you have settled *what* you want to communicate *to whom* and *why*.

AND FINALLY . . .

Regardless of how careful you are when developing evidence-based questions, frameworks, and designs, or how much experience you have working in a field, the best insights often come from experiencing what happens when a design stalls or a question doesn't work.

Even though you may have taken a comprehensive, collaborative approach, sometimes the discussion and decision-making process clearly reveal that it was the wrong question or that it needed to be tweaked to be effective. As with most things in life, you need to be engaged in these processes that tend to have uncertain outcomes several times to really feel comfortable with the inherent tension.

17

17

What sustains us as process consultants is knowing that building designs and questions collaboratively, based on the best evidence available, contains the possibility of evidence-based answers that have the potential to change how things are done for the betterment of people's lives.

PROPOSITIONS

62. The answer is not in the question: the question points toward an answer by identifying a decision to be made. The answer points toward implementation challenges. The implementation challenges in turn raise new questions. And so it goes with process consultation.

63. It takes an intelligent, focused, and committed leader to ride the rigor required to create great questions collaboratively.

64. Unconventional thinkers question the conventional—a necessary element in evidence-based process design.

65. The best evidence-based designs encourage, protect, and reward risk takers.

5 SAMPLE PROCESS DESIGNS

Part Five offers two sector-specific examples of process designs: one for a private corporation, and the other for a nongovernment organization.

These designs are based on the concepts provided in the first three parts of this book: taking a stepwise approach, addressing people factors, and completing a PTR to support due diligence.

Each design is customized to fit the unique demands of a PTR developed collaboratively with stakeholders. As a result, several models or technologies for facilitation are integrated in each design. To avoid jargon, specific models, technologies, approaches, and frameworks are not named in these designs: instead, a detailed outline is provided. This integrated use of a range of technologies, models, approaches, and tools is the essence of a customized approach to process design.

18

A Town Hall Meeting with XYZ Finance Department

Client: XYZ (North American Finance Department in a global bank)

Time available: 8:00 A.M.–1:30 P.M.

Participants: Planning committee members (8 including VP Finance) and all staff; total of 235

Location: Off-site conference center near headquarters

Purpose: Celebrate, share information, and continue to create teamwork in Finance

- Next year's objectives for XYZ Finance and Divisional Finance
- Celebrating what is right in the world
  - Previous year's XYZ Finance accomplishments
  - XYZ Finance Townhall Awards
  - Next year's objectives: XYZ Finance and Divisional Finance
  - XYZ Finance top common behavioral changes for next year
  - XYZ Finance organization announcements

Desired Outcomes:

- Create a shared understanding of XYZ Finance objectives for the upcoming year
- Create a shared understanding of XYZ Finance divisional objectives for the upcoming year

- Create a mind-set for required behavioral changes in XYZ Finance: what does this look like?

- Focus on moving forward: announcement of XYZ Finance organization design work

18

Time	Item	Who
8:00–8:20 A.M.	Breakfast—Skytower Room—interaction and socialization.	Anne and David set each table and are on hand to help out. Jane places packages of handouts, noise makers, and other items on tables before hall doors open.
8:20–8:30 A.M.	Doors open—music playing—"Taking Care of Business"—clips from our various celebrations, and so on.	George produces.
	Prearranged seating—mixed participants from each Finance area at each table—includes names from Succession Planning at specific tables. Departmental leaders assigned to specific tables. Post names for seating on flip chart paper (something big) at the table near the Hall entrance.	Jane organizes seating.
	Greeters from each department at the door to welcome participants.	Facilitator organizes greeters at hall doors.

Time	Item	Who
8:30–8:35 A.M.	Welcome speech—explain theme of celebration: why this, why now.	VP Finance
	Facilitator briefly reviews agenda flow, assumptions, and key considerations.	Facilitator creates Power-Point highlights on the agenda flow.
8:35–8:40 A.M.	Picture presentation: collage of Zander's photos with music. Energize the audience; get the tempo up.	George (producer) will test out on Sunday beforehand to ensure technical setup as outlined in the agenda.
8:40–8:45 A.M.	Celebration practice—participants grab a noise maker from the table and make noise—try it out—we're getting ready to celebrate.	Facilitator leads the celebration practice.
8:45–9:00 A.M.	Celebrate past 12 months' accomplishments (15 min). Review objectives met.	VP Finance group prepares material and reviews it with audience. VP Finance introduces Success Champions for Finance (two award winners).
9:00–9:05 A.M.	Success Champions talk about how the work got done, focusing on teamwork and behaviors. Champion #1—focus on "Being a Strong Unified Leadership Team" and "Commitment to our High Performance	Chosen Success Champions weave their personal stories into the presentations.

(continued on next page)

18

Time	Item	Who
	Team"—uses examples of activities participated in—for example, Out of the Cold.	
	Champion #2—focus on Operations Effectiveness and how objectives were achieved.	
9:05–9:15 A.M.	Celebrate XYZ Finance Awards: Last year's award winners present awards to one employee at a time—twelve employees: Employee comes on stage and receives $100 cash. George (producer) cues music to accompany award winners as they walk up to the stage. Audience shows appreciation with noise makers. Award winners stay on stage; Facilitator helps shepherd employees to the side.	Two of last year's award winners introduce new award recipients. Fundraising committee secures money to cover costs. AV group prepares awards—slides and envelopes. George is producer for this segment.
9:15–9:45 A.M.	Toast our accomplishments. 10 minutes table work to create a toast. 10 minutes—large group hears the toasts—roaming microphone. Show instruction slide on PowerPoint. Guidelines for Toasts • Four lines • Rhythm	Facilitator: • Prepares audience and does debrief. • Advises audience of instruction sheet on the table. • Advises audience that glasses are being handed out and not to drink until instructed.

18

Time	Item	Who
	• Rhyme • Wit and humor • Highlight an accomplishment—what or how 10 minutes—instructions and flex time.	Sidenote: While groups are working on their toast, servers will place the glasses on the table.
9:45–10:00 A.M.	BREAK	Facilitator announces break and more excitement to follow.
10:00–10:30 A.M.	Video—"Celebrating What Is Right in the World." Two Senior Directors describe the video, which features the work of National Geographic photographer Dewitt Jones and helps us start to think about celebrating what is possible. View video (20 min). Discuss the video and the seven key themes (8 min). "The seven themes that came out of the video are:" (Facilitator to read out themes). Dialogue between Senior Directors: Which theme resonated for you? (#1 to elaborate). Which themes resonated for you? (#2 to elaborate).	Senior Directors: • Introduce video. • Reflect on what they got out of the video when they first viewed it at the Leadership Working Session six months ago. Use one of the seven key themes to illustrate impact. Themes: • Believe it and you will see it. • Recognize abundance. • Look for possibilities. • Unleash your energy to fix what's wrong. • Ride the changes. • Take yourself to the edge. • Be your best for the world.

18

(continued on next page)

Time	Item	Who
	Take one minute at your tables and think about what resonated for each of you and discuss with the person sitting next to you.	
	Keep your thoughts, because we will need to think about themes and how we will be able to apply them in the future.	
	Speaking about the future, our VP Finance is going to share with us our 2009 objectives and going forward on our journey.	
10:30–11:00 A.M.	XYZ Finance 2009 Objectives	VP Finance
	Where we're headed.	Facilitator: preps and facilitates—Time to reflect for 5–10 minutes.
	Update on leadership working session.	
	Organizational changes.	At tables let employees take a few minutes to digest what has been communicated.
	Link to XYZ Finance journey.	
	Announce organization changes; acknowledge compassionately that managers have talked to employees— some happy, some unsure, some worried. Any change is a big change—let's support each other through this.	
	VP Finance weaves in a story about the org announcement and feelings surrounding the changes.	
11:00–11:45 A.M.	Group Team behaviors	Facilitator reviews exercise and facilitates session.
	Each person receives a page with the 2009 objectives on it	Facilitator creates examples.

Time	Item	Who
	on one side and the key concepts on the other side. What is one thing (change) you could do personally to help XYZ Finance move in the right direction? (2–3 min). Discuss at table. Table identifies one or two common changes for a report back to the group. Guidelines around the **what** is it—(behaviors that others will see or hear—need some examples) (15 min). Large group report back from each table (20 min).	Zander prepares instructions and the one-pager with last year's objectives and key concepts—note that Scribe, Timekeeper, and Reporter are required from each table. Zander prepares worksheet for employees at their tables to use to record their team's two common changes. He explains to audience that we will collect this information to help create our XYZ Finance Brand. We will post information on the Finance Evolution Web site.
11:45–12:00 P.M.	Closure: Thank the Townhall Planning Committee. Recap—Outstanding work "Taking Care of Business."	VP Finance and Facilitator do a wrap-up—what we achieved in the Townhall.
12:00–1:30 P.M.	Lunch in the Dungeon Include stories from Direct Reports. People leave when they are ready.	Facilitator announces lunch. The three recognized staff need to have their personal stories ready. They chat for 3 minutes each—be informal, passionate, and interesting—focus on who you are versus what you do at work. Stimulate conversation at tables.

18

A Workshop on Mission and Values

Client: Strategic Planning Department in a national charity

Time available: One day

Participants: Eleven national board members, thirteen state presidents, six senior national staff, ten state senior staff for a total of forty

Location: Large off-site conference center to accommodate people sitting at tables of eight in half-rounds facing the front of the room

Version: Working Design, Draft #2

Accountability: To support objectivity, the process consultant is the main facilitator and accountable for design items unless indicated otherwise.

DRAFT DESIGN #2 FOR PLANNING COMMITTEE REVIEW

8:30 A.M. Check room setup: five tables of eight participants in half-rounds facing the front.	Name tags in alpha order: who at registration? Extra copies of background documents. On tables: agenda, norms. Flip charts and markers. DS bring dictionaries. Check on group setup with PMT.

(continued on next page)

9:00 A.M.
Meeting of
Planning Group—
clarify their roles
during the
workshop.
	• Flow of the agenda: four parts
	• Opening remarks by national president
	  • Welcome
	  • History, evolution of the federation, decision
	  • Steps in the process
	  • Fiduciary responsibilities
	  • Introduction of planning group members
	  • Key messages:
	    National strategic perspective
	    Inclusive approach
	    Celebrating that our NGO is a mission-driven organization
	    Collaboration not advocacy for a single state's perspective
	    Staged implementation
	  • Praxis (explain) at the heart of both mission and values: policy into action.
	• Values are in place whether they are stated or not: task is to make explicit what is implicit.
	• Decision was made to move this forward; don't re-make the decision.
	• Who is the target for the mission statement—the public?
	• Key Terms (to avoid confusion in discussions):
	  • *Federation:* An organization or group within which smaller divisions have some degree of internal autonomy; root word is from Latin: *foederare*—to ally; defined through practice, for example, European Union/Community.
	  • *Federation Board.*
	  • *Federation Office.*
	  • Refer to definitions of *mission, vision, values;* emphasize the need to move from posted to operative values.

19

9:50 A.M. Registration (informal) and pick up name tags (HR department organizes; support staff at registration table).	
10:00 A.M. Opening Remarks: NGO President	Background: excerpt from the strategic plan (PowerPoint): "The work of the federation will be strengthened and made more consistent through the development and application by all partners of one set of guiding principles, one shared mission statement, one set of values, and a clear definition of roles and responsibilities. These will become the fundamental underpinnings and tenets on which all federation work is based. In the next fiscal year, a facilitated workshop of our board, state foundation chairs, and state executive directors will be held to develop the shared mission statement, principles and values. An aligned planning process across the federation will be introduced by year three."
10:05 A.M. Purpose: Facilitator	• To develop a draft shared statement of mission and values. • To develop a process for federation members to review the draft and move to adoption. This is not a crisis situation; it's ongoing business in following through on the strategic plan. Flow of the agenda: Part I: Missions and Values Across the Country Part II: A Mission Statement for the Federation Part III: Values for the Federation Part IV: Implementation *Introductions* (20 seconds each) • Name, affiliation • From your perspective, and based on your experience with this federation, what needs to happen at this workshop to make it a success?

19

(continued on next page)

	Plenary question: When you look at your responses, what are the implications for this workshop?
	Norms for working together: match the cartoons to the guidelines (provides continuity and reinforcement because used in other NGO workshops).
	To do a good job on mission and values, need to have a comfortable, nonthreatening climate with clear expectations about how people will work together. Norms can be helpful with this.
	1. Share the airtime.
	2. Collaborate to reach agreement.
	3. Think national and strategic.
	4. Explore perspectives.
	5. Don't overlook the simple or the obvious.
	Are we missing any norms that need to be addressed based on what you said in your introductions?
10:30 A.M. Part I: Missions and Values Across the Country	Background Document comparing missions and values (go through by major sections—10 minutes):
	• First page: how developed.
	• Number of responses: twenty-two of forty.
	• Kick-start for discussion; not final word.
	• Document was developed and synthesized based on what was said, not on who said what; sorting was based on key language.
	• Numbers are based on your description; if your state said its submission was from three workshop participants then it was counted as three.
	Plenary discussion: What stands out?
11:00 A.M. Part II: A Mission Statement for the Federation (FC)	Review and confirm the definition of mission in the background document (page 2).
	Distinguish among mission, mandate, logo.
	Clarify that the mission statement is for a federation rather than a foundation and discuss related implications.

19

Ask about areas of obvious agreement in the background document.

Table work: use the background document as a start (pages 3–5) and focus on a federation-wide perspective:

1. Review current statements, analysis, and survey results.

2. Come to agreement on a draft mission statement for the federation and put it on your table's flip chart.

    Stem: "The mission of the federation is to . . .

    Include room to dance, that is, room for the required small variations among states that were outlined in the background document.

3. Ask the test question (see page 6): Does this mission statement have embedded in it what makes us unique?

• Process the drafts in plenary session, building agreement through consensus. Begin with participants posting all their suggested mission statements together on the long side wall. Ask everyone to stand and move toward the long side wall where they can see all five suggestions at once.

    • Remind group re the need to collaborate on a common statement and the norms required to do that.

    • Ask about obvious areas of similarity.

    • Ask which two or three statements seem to embrace the federation.

    • Continue to build a consensus on the front wall.

19

12:30 P.M.
Lunch (to be ready at 12:15 P.M. for possible early finish).

(continued on next page)

19

1:15 P.M. Part III: Values for the Federation	• Review and clarify key terms: levels of values, praxis, evolution over time, posted to operative—see document. • Discuss how difficult it is to implement high-level values—not a matter of quick answers; need to be interpreted; example of Cheney case and shooting of friend. • Conduct this part of the session as follows: *Table work:* using the background document as a start, develop a draft set of values for the federation: individuals jot down top three then share at tables and come to consensus. *Plenary:* come to agreement on list of values: start with top value for each table and continue until all exhausted. *Table work:* Assign one value per table for a one- or two-sentence description. *Task:* Add a descriptive sentence, for example, We . . . . (Use the definitions in the back of the background document as a starting point.) • Process the drafts in plenary session: focus on building agreement. • Flip chart the values and descriptions—one per table and per flip chart.
2:30 P.M. Break	
2:45 P.M. Part IV: Implementation	• Prepare *Guidelines for Working Together* in the federation, for example, norms over the long term (time allotted will depend on how previous parts of the agenda flow; mission and values are top two priorities). • Emphasize that these guidelines are like standard operating procedures: how we do business on a day-to-day basis. • Roles and responsibilities will be clear and people will work within them.

- Policies once approved are federation policies; they can't be shelved or ignored at the state level, but if they aren't working they need to be flagged and reviewed at the federation level to make them workable.

- Members should share learning and best practices, not be too proprietary with what they know and have.

- State orientation of volunteers should include orientation to the federation so that senior volunteers know they are part of a broader federation.

- Review and confirm the above in plenary.

- Action Steps—Table Task: Question

  The initial idea was that mission and values would subsequently be adopted by all federation members (states) effective November 1 this year. Given that states are at different stages in the development and ownership of mission and values, how could the implementation happen in a respectful and efficient manner?

  When considering this question, think about the PIE response: to what extent do we need to persuade, inform, or engage the states on this initiative?

- Process the results in plenary based on group reports.

- Over to the Federation CEO for implementation.

- *If time allows, ask,* "Now that we have developed a shared mission and values, how can we continue to align ourselves on other aspects of how we work together?

4:20 P.M.
Concluding
Remarks: National
president

4:30 P.M.
Closing

19

References

Adkins, Jennifer, and others. *Diversity Education for Change: A Guide to Planning and Management.* Calgary, Alberta: Plan:Net Limited, 2004. Available online: http://tprc.alberta.ca/humanrights/publications/diversity/default.aspx. Access date: November 7, 2007.

Annie E. Casey Foundation. *Local Learning Partnership Guidebook,* Chapter 4: "Issues That Cut Across All Types of Data Activities." Baltimore: Annie E. Casey Foundation, 2002. Available online: www.yepp-community.org/downloads/empowerment/LLPguidebook.pdf. Access date: December 29, 2007.

Baldwin, S. As quoted in Gray, Barbara. *Collaborating.* San Francisco: Jossey-Bass, 1989, p. 95.

Bryson, J. M. *Strategic Planning for Public and Nonprofit Organizations: A Guide to Strengthening and Sustaining Organizational Achievement.* San Francisco: Jossey-Bass, 1988.

ChangingMinds.org. "SMART Objectives." Available online: http://changingminds.org/disciplines/hr/performance_management/smart_objectives.htm. Access date: November 7, 2007.

Cohen, R. *The Good, the Bad and the Difference.* New York: Broadway Books, 2002.

Cuming, P. *The Power Handbook: A Strategic Guide to Organizational and Personal Effectiveness.* Toronto: Van Nostrand Reinhold, 1981.

Davies, Philip T. "Is Evidence-Based Government Possible?" Jerry Lee Lecture, 2004. Available online: www.policyhub.gov.uk/downloads/JerryLeeLecture1202041.pdf. Access date: December 29, 2007.

Dillard, Annie. *Living by Fiction.* New York: HarperCollins, 1982.

Gray, B. *Collaborating: Finding Common Ground for Multiparty Problems.* San Francisco: Jossey-Bass, 1989.

Grimshaw, J. M., and others. "Effectiveness and Efficiency of Guideline Dissemination and Implementation, Strategies." *Health Technology Assessment,* 2004, *8*(6). Available online: www.ncchta.org/execsumm/summ806.htm. Access date: December 29, 2007.

Hayakawa, S. I. *Language in Thought and Action.* New York: First Harvest, 1990. (Originally published 1939.)

Hodgkinson, C. *The Philosophy of Leadership.* Oxford, England: Basil Blackwell, 1983.

Hodgkinson, C. *Educational Leadership: The Moral Art.* Albany: State University of New York Press, 1991.

Hodgkinson, C. *Administrative Philosophy: Values and Motivations in Administrative Life.* Oxford, England: Elsevier Science, 1996.

"IDEA Project (Innovation, Development, Employment, Applications)." Economic Development Concept Workshop and Discussion Forum, March 2000. Available online: www .ideaproject.com.au/public/workshop. Access date: November 7, 2007.

Institute on Governance. "Practical Problems and Solutions: Stakeholders and Accountability," n.d. Available online: www.iog.ca/boardgovernance/html/pra_key_sta.html. Access date: November 7, 2007.

Janis, Irving L. *Groupthink: Psychological Studies of Policy Decisions and Fiascoes* (2nd ed.). New York: Houghton Mifflin, 1982.

Kitzmiller, M. H. "Bases of Power: Developing the Group's Potential," in *The 1991 Annual: Developing Human Resources.* San Diego, Calif.: University Associates, 1991.

Knoll, Gregg, and others. *Kidney Allocation in Canada: A Canadian Forum.* Edmonton, Alberta: Canadian Council for Donation and Transplantation, 2007. Available online: www.ccdt.ca/english/publications/final.html#KA. Access date: December 18, 2007.

Martin, R. "A Progress Report on Integrative Thinking." Toronto: Joseph L. Rotman School of Management, University of Toronto, promotional brochure, n.d., p. 2. Available online: www.rotman.utoronto.ca/integrativethinking.htm. Access date: December 18, 2007.

OpenClinical. "Evidence-Based Medicine," January 7, 2007. Available online: www.open clinical.org/ebm.html. Access date: November 14, 2007.

Schein, E. H. *Process Consultation,* Vol. 2. Reading, Mass.: Addison-Wesley, 1987.

Schumacher, E. F. *A Guide for the Perplexed.* New York: HarperCollins, 1977.

Schuman, S. (ed.). *Creating a Culture of Collaboration.* San Francisco: Jossey-Bass, 2006.

262

Senge, P. *The Fifth Discipline: The Art and Practice of the Learning Organization.* New York: Doubleday/Currency, 1990.

Senge, P., Kleiner, A., Roberts, C., Ross, R., and Smith, B. *The Fifth Discipline Fieldbook: Strategies and Tools for Building a Learning Organization.* New York: Doubleday/Currency, 1994.

Shookner, M. *Inclusion Lens: Workbook for Looking at Social and Economic Exclusion and Inclusion.* Public Health Agency of Canada, Atlantic Canada, 2002. Available online: www.phac-aspc.gc.ca/canada/regions/atlantic/Publications/Inclusion_lens/index.html. Access date: November 7, 2007.

Strachan, D. *Making Questions Work: A Guide to What and How to Ask for Facilitators, Consultants, Managers, Coaches, and Educators.* San Francisco: Jossey-Bass, 2007.

Stybel, L. J., and Peabody, M. "Friend, Foe, Ally, Adversary . . . or Something Else?" *MIT Sloan Management Review,* Summer 2005, pp. 15–16.

Taylor, Charles. *Philosophical Arguments.* Cambridge, Mass.: Harvard University Press, 1995.

Tomlinson, P., and Strachan, D. *Power and Ethics in Coaching.* Ottawa: Coaching Association of Canada, 1996.

Tomlinson, P., and Strachan, D. *A Guide to Collaborative Processes in Health Policy Development and Their Implications for Action.* Ottawa: VOICE in health policy project, Canadian Public Health Association, 2005. Available online: www.projectvoice.ca. Access date: November 7, 2007.

Tuckman, B. W. "Development Sequence in Small Groups." *American Psychological Association, Psychological Bulletin,* 1965, *63*(6), 384–399.

Voluntary Sector Initiative, Canada: Joint Accord Table. "A Code of Good Practice on Policy Dialogue: Building on an Accord Between the Government of Canada and the Voluntary Sector," October 2002. Available online: www.vsi-isbc.org/eng/policy/policy_code.cfm. Access date: November 7, 2007.

Wilder, L. I. *Little Town on the Prairie.* New York: HarperCollins, 1953.

Winer, M. B., and Ray, K. L. *Collaboration Handbook: Creating, Sustaining, and Enjoying the Journey.* St. Paul, Minn.: Amherst H. Wilder Foundation, 1994.